T0355946

Praise for
The Rainmaker Multiplier

"There's a reason why so many advisors look to Jason L Smith for guidance to run a successful advisory business. First, he's done it himself. His own business continues to grow and thrive. Second, Jason has a knack for explaining his success principles in a way that other advisors can run with. *The Rainmaker Multiplier* will become a reference book to any advisor wishing for sustained success."

—Bill Cates, president, Referral Coach International

"As a business owner, you only have so much time to build a business that will grow for years to come, so the only way to do that is to leverage your time. Jason Smith's *The Rainmaker Multiplier* gives you the tools to do just that. Use them and watch what happens!"

—Ed Slott, CPA, founder, irahelp.com

"This book is an important read for any financial advisory business owner striving to build something bigger than themselves that will stand the test of time. The Rainmaker Multiplier process has the proven scalability to take aspirational advisors to the next level. Jason is the real deal, and his personal story of growing his business is beyond inspiring; this book is the road map for you to do the same."

—Chad Johnson, chief inspiration officer, The Giant 5 Guy

"I've worked with hundreds of business owners that want to scale but don't know how without being able to clone themselves. Jason Smith's *The Rainmaker Multiplier* is an essential read for any financial service business owner or advisor that wants to scale, grow, and have true impact. Jason's story is inspiring, and this groundbreaking guide provides a proven process to scale your business by scaling yourself and your passion, enabling your business to thrive. Smith's insights are both transformative and practical, making this book an invaluable resource for anyone looking to elevate their business to new heights."

—Jamie P. Hopkins, chief wealth officer and CEO, Bryn Mawr Trust

"Jason Smith's book offers a good blueprint for creating a successful advisory business that functions as a true ensemble organization that does not over-rely on the talent and knowledge of one person. But Jason does more than that; he tells a captivating and very personal story that is inspiring and instructional. Watching him build his life, his practice, and his business one decision at a time and one relationship at a time is something every entrepreneur can relate to and something every aspiring new advisor can learn from. Jason is hungry for knowledge, to do better for clients, to succeed, to do well for his family, to experience life—and that thirst makes the book not just instructional but also very relatable and inspirational."

—Philip Palaveev, CEO, The Ensemble Practice

THE RAINMAKER
MULTIPLIER

How to Create a Self-Sustaining, Scalable Financial Planning Business

JASON L SMITH

GREENLEAF
BOOK GROUP PRESS

Published by Greenleaf Book Group Press
Austin, Texas
www.gbgpress.com

Distributed by Greenleaf Book Group

For ordering information or special discounts for bulk purchases, please contact Greenleaf Book Group at PO Box 91869, Austin, TX 78709, 512.891.6100.

Design and composition by Greenleaf Book Group and Mimi Bark
Cover design by Greenleaf Book Group and Mimi Bark
Cover images used under license from ©Shutterstock.com/ASAG Studio

Publisher's Cataloging-in-Publication data is available.

Print ISBN: 979-8-88645-181-8

eBook ISBN: 979-8-88645-182-5

To offset the number of trees consumed in the printing of our books, Greenleaf donates a portion of the proceeds from each printing to the Arbor Day Foundation. Greenleaf Book Group has replaced over 50,000 trees since 2007.

Printed in the United States of America on acid-free paper

25 26 27 28 29 30 31 32   10 9 8 7 6 5 4 3 2 1

First Edition

For my fearless wife, Holly,
who believes in me beyond reason.

To Jeff Warnkin, the humble hero who
helped make this story possible.

Contents

PART III: Choose Your Own Adventure: RMM Building Blocks

Foreword by Dan Sullivan

Jason L Smith is a particularly impressive example of a future-savvy financial advisor who stands out in my experience since I started coaching successful entrepreneurs in 1974.

He's proven that he can transform his own advisory practice by 100x in less than twenty years.

His advisory firm is designed to attract and transform committed clientele who are eager for long-term financial coaching.

He's systematically transformed his best success strategies into timeless processes that enable thousands of like-minded advisors to prosper.

A bit of background to explain why these three achievements and capabilities of Jason's are so important right now—and going forward in the twenty-first century:

I was born in 1944, two weeks before the Normandy Invasion that accelerated the ending of the worst war in history. I was born six weeks before the Bretton Woods Conference that essentially created the global economy for the next seventy-five years. And my present coaching career began in 1974, right when futurists started talking about a tiny new invention called the microchip.

Most successful financial advisors active today and their clientele have lived in a globally peaceful world, one that has been propelled forward by an ever-expanding global economy and one in which microchip-based technologies are continually producing greater prosperity.

That's been the story for my whole life and for virtually everyone I know. Until 2020. That's when a lot of things started to change in confusing and disruptive ways—mostly in negative ways, and increasingly in scary, new ways that many smart, experienced financial advisors and their successful, well-off clientele hadn't prepared for and didn't know how to think about.

This is where Jason L Smith's approach and contribution come into the spotlight. What he's achieved, and what he's offering in this book, is crucially important for financial advisors and their clientele who are clear that the world has changed in a very short time and that things are not going back to "normal."

The world is about to become even more confusing and conflicted—unpredictable, unequal, and a lot more complicated.

Jason knows this is true for his own company and clientele, and he's spent the last two decades constructing a foundation that remains solid, simple, and timeless, regardless of how shaky and unpredictable the world outside becomes.

His purpose and goal from now on is to share his time-tested strategies, structures, and processes with many others. This book is a great read for anyone who's aiming to be successful in a new world that is already disrupting into something that most people still aren't expecting.

Dan Sullivan
Co-founder and president of Strategic Coach®

If you are a successful advisor looking for a proven formula for multiplying yourself as a rainmaker . . . if you are a person who is dedicated to education and growth . . . someone who wants to advance and invest wisely in your practice and your family's future, then you've come to the right place. This book is for you.

Let's Start with the "Why"

It had been a long night, the longest in my forty-one years on this planet. I'd been tossing and turning in bed for hours with no sleep. I rolled to my right and opened my eyes. The digital clock glowed neon blue in the darkness of our room: *4:37 a.m.* I rolled to my left and sighed. I had only twenty-three minutes before the alarm went off so my wife, Holly, and I could make it to the hospital in time for my open-heart surgery, the surgery I'd known for years was going to happen someday. Today was the day. In the clock's glow I could see Holly—seven months pregnant with twins—sleeping soundly beside me, and a huge wave of love washed over me. *You've got to be strong for her and the kids*, I told myself. *Just relax and be brave. You'll be right back here in this bed in a couple of days, and back to work in no time.*

A few hours later I was in an operating room surrounded by my new best friends: the surgical team at Cleveland Clinic that would be taking care of me for the foreseeable future. As they bustled around getting everything ready, I did my best to convince myself that this was no big deal. I even cracked a few jokes to lighten the mood.

"Man, you seem so calm," said one of the nurses. "What's your secret?"

"You know what? I feel good," I replied. "I have everything in place. No matter what happens today, it's going to be okay."

He nodded and patted my arm, the anesthesiologist knocked me out, and the next thing I remember, I woke up paralyzed, doctors and nurses shouting frantically all around me. I couldn't open my eyes and I couldn't talk or move, yet I could hear and understand everything that was going on around me. "We have a heartbeat!" somebody shouted.

I realized they were talking about me. I had flatlined on the operating table.

I now tuned in to the distress of two people in the ICU beds beside me. Nurses yelled, "Hang in there! Squeeze my hand!" followed by the sound of defibrillator paddles hitting the patients and then the noise of the flatline on their monitors. It was horrendous, like being in a living nightmare. I tried with all my might to wake myself up, but I couldn't.

I lived in that hell for the next two days. I wondered if anyone was tending to me, as they all seemed to avoid trying to do something to fix me.

What should have been six hours under anesthesia had turned into fifty-two hours. I found out later that the medical team had tried to bring me out of it, but my heart went into ventricular tachycardia (or v-tach), meaning it would beat extremely rapidly and abnormally. That can cause sudden death, so they decided not to push me and just let me continue to sleep.

When I finally did wake up completely, I was relieved but

confused. I tried to jump out of bed to figure out what was going on, but the massive number of tubes everywhere—I think I counted sixteen of them—prevented me from moving. In my raspy voice, I told the nurses not to let Holly come into the room because I didn't want her to see me like that. I was frantic, nervous, and anxious to get a grasp on reality. The nurses kept encouraging me to relax and go back to sleep, but I told them hell no, I had just come out of a paralyzed nightmare and was not going to risk going back there.

Two days later, while my sister Kim was visiting me in the ICU, alarms started going off on my monitor. I felt dizzy. The doctor who had just left my room thirty seconds before rushed back in, checked the machine, and said I had gone into v-tach again. While monitoring my condition, he turned to Kim as the representative of our family.

"I'm afraid this is not good," he said. "Your brother needs to consider saying his goodbyes."

Kim and I just looked at each other like, "*What?*" Seriously, how do you process that kind of information? The way we handled it was to do what the doctor ordered. Kim helped me call our mom and tell her goodbye. You can imagine what that was like. I called my daughter Jordan, who was away at college, and told her goodbye. Again, soul crushing. Holly rushed in, and I was wheeled over to the only private room in the ICU, which I figured out is where they take you when you're about to die. The nurses gave me all kinds of meds to try to knock me out so my body could relax, but I fought giving in. They and the doctors pleaded with me to close my eyes and rest, as that would give me the best chance of making it through, but I refused to allow my body to shut down. Ultimately, though, I did follow their advice. I said goodbye to Holly and she said goodbye to me. The last thing I remember is her beautiful face and her holding my hand. I fell asleep believing that this was the end.

And then, six hours later, I woke up. Turns out it wasn't the end after all (in case you hadn't guessed by now). The surgery had not been successful, but at least I was still alive. It turned out that I had a hereditary heart condition that my grandmother also had, and she lived to be ninety-three.

At the conclusion of a lengthy hospital stay, my doctors told me that I could not go back to work for a while . . . a long while. They wanted me in a zero-stress environment until my heart settled down and I got stronger. In preparation for the surgery, I had turned over my office cell phone to my team—every connection to the outside world including all links to my successful holistic wealth management practice, JL Smith. I even told my team leaders not to contact me so I could recover in peace.

"I don't care if the SEC and the IRS [US Securities and Exchange Commission and the Internal Revenue Service] are beating down our door," I said. "I don't care if the building is burning to the ground. *Don't call me.*"

Little did I know that they would be following that directive for the next several months. Whereas I thought I'd be off work for about two weeks after my surgery, I was out for five months. Five months! And not simply "out" but totally disconnected . . . completely off the grid. No business texts, no calls, no meetings, no emails. To have no clue what was happening in the business I had fought so hard to build—to have no touchpoints with my team and my clients for that many months—felt absolutely crazy.

Turns out it was a blessing in disguise, though, because it was a stress test of the model that I had been teaching other financial advisors for nearly a decade. This was the ultimate proof of concept: *Was it possible to create a thriving holistic wealth management practice that would survive with or without me, that would provide security for my family and continuity for my clients if something were to happen to me?* I might never have known the answer to that question had I not had a health crisis that forced me to find out.

> "Sometimes the bad things that happen in our lives put us directly on the path to the best things that will ever happen to us."
>
> **—NICOLE REED**

THE VERDICT

I was a bit nervous on my first day back to work after all those long months away. I had no idea what the financial situation was with JL Smith. Were we running out of money? Had we maxed out the credit cards? Had all our best clients bailed on us? I did not know. I found Bryan, an up-and-coming advisor you will hear more about in the pages ahead, waiting for me in my office. His facial expression was somber. I sat down across the desk from him and exhaled.

"All right, Bryan, give it to me straight," I said. "Where are we at?"

Bryan shook his head and looked away. "I don't know how to tell you this," he mumbled.

I felt that sinking sensation in my gut . . . the one I always get when I'm about to be hit with bad news. "Come on, what is it?" I replied. "Just tell me."

Suddenly a huge grin flashed across Bryan's face and he blurted out, "WE CRUSHED IT! We had the second most profitable quarter *ever!*"

"You've got to be kidding me," I said. "Don't joke about this, Bryan."

"No, I'm dead serious, man. Look." He brought up the profit and loss statement (P&L) on the computer, and there it was . . . the second-best set of numbers in the history of the company. My jaw dropped, and it took me a second to find my voice.

"Huh. Wow," I said, staring at the P&L in disbelief. I turned to Bryan, who could barely contain his excitement.

"All righty then," I said with a shrug. "I guess this means you guys don't need me anymore? Guess my work here is done . . . guess I'll just pack up my things and go . . . ride off into the sunset . . ."

Bryan laughed. I was joking, but just barely. There it was in black and white. My business truly didn't need me to be the rainmaker anymore.

. . . .

Think about what your business would look like if you had to take off for five months like I did. Can you say with confidence that you have the right processes and people in place to sustain growth in your absence? Do you have total confidence in your business's sustainability and succession plan should something happen to you? In the early years of building my business, I asked myself these same questions, and the answer was a resounding "NO," not by a long shot. If something had happened to me during those years, if I had died on the operating table at that time, my income would have died with me, and my wife and kids would have been in bad shape as a result.

My heart surgery experience inspired me mentally, physically, and spiritually. It made me stronger and gave me the confidence I never would have had if not for these life-altering events. I first got the diagnosis of my heart condition at age twenty-nine, and starting then I set out to build a practice that would run profitably with or without me, and not just survive but thrive in my absence.

Over the ensuing eleven years leading up to my surgery, a model was born for how to do that: The Rainmaker Multiplier. This is the very same model that made it possible for my business to run—and succeed magnificently—without me even being there. In short, the concept is that instead of one advisor bringing in all the business, several advisors are trained on the right processes (power of people plus process), thus multiplying their efforts.

WHY THE MODEL WORKS

The silo approach to financial planning—working with an investment advisor, an insurance professional, a tax planner, and an attorney individually, without collaboration—is becoming an outdated model for the history books. The modern model of holistic planning brings the services of the investment advisor, insurance professional, tax planner, and attorney together, all working collaboratively on the client's behalf with you serving as the coach, quarterback, or household financial CFO or point guard, ensuring that no balls get dropped.

Holistic planning is not a new concept, but it has traditionally been reserved for ultra-high-net-worth families. Firms like Goldman Sachs and boutique family offices have provided holistic planning to those clients, but the mass affluent American families have been largely neglected. Instead, these hardworking families and individuals who have accumulated significant wealth have traditionally been served by professionals working in isolation, largely acting as salespeople rather than holistic advisors. It doesn't matter if the professionals are selling stocks, bonds, life insurance policies, annuities, wills or trusts, or selling tax preparation or accounting services. They are all just selling products and services specific to their professions. Rarely are they tying it all together into one comprehensive holistic plan. That's what the holistic planning process does. I wrote a book about our process entitled *The Bucket Plan: Protecting and Growing Your Assets for a Worry-Free Retirement*,[1] in which I described how the planning process works from a client-facing perspective.

For the purposes of this book, I want to emphasize that holistic planning is a core foundational part of becoming a rainmaker, or the one who brings in the business, because it helps you systematize and professionalize your service delivery while simultaneously fulfilling your fiduciary duty to your clients. But holistic planning alone is not enough to sustain and grow a profitable practice for the long haul. You can be the greatest holistic planner in the world, but if you have difficulty getting in front of new people via proven marketing and referral systems; fail to diversify your income streams by pursuing various profitable business lines; and/or don't have a process for hiring, training, and advancing new advisors (an advisor career path), then you will not be able to scale your business. It will always depend on you—and only you—to keep the wheels turning. I happen to think there's more to life than that . . . especially when there's no exit ramp in sight.

For that reason we created the Rainmaker Multiplier (RMM) Proven Process and Platform to help advisors build thriving, sustainable, holistic wealth management practices that truly serve the best interests of their ideal clients. This book tells the true story of

---

1   Jason L Smith, *The Bucket Plan: Protecting and Growing Your Assets for a Worry-Free Retirement* (Austin, TX: Greenleaf, 2017).

how I built a practice that provides security for my family and runs seamlessly without me even being there, and gives you many of the concepts and tools to start doing the same.

WHAT'S AHEAD?

In Part I you'll read about my motivation for developing the RMM Proven Process and Platform and meet the two advisors—one an industry veteran and the other a rookie fresh out of college—who provided the energy, drive, and spark to help me multiply my effect as the sole income producer. They are the real heroes of this story—which is a true story, by the way. My hope is that Part I will inspire you to think about your own path toward building a self-sustaining, profitable practice that can and will grow even if you step away. By the time you finish reading Part I, you'll probably realize that you've been laying the groundwork for a self-sustaining practice for years . . . you just didn't know it!

In Part II we'll touch upon the four essential elements for building a practice that thrives with you or without you:

- The holistic planning process
- Adding (or growing) a tax planning, management, and preparation element to your business
- Creating a marketing strategy and executing a plan
- Implementing a proven career path for the current and future advisors in your firm

You will get the secret sauce to the process for increasing your revenue and client base by charging planning fees—a process that increases your perceived value and attracts ideal clients, those with a high net worth—who are happy to pay you to share the knowledge and wisdom you've accumulated. Part of that secret sauce includes access to an online resource that walks you through how we run the first step of The Bucket Plan* holistic planning process to put clients on the path to a secure retirement. Even if you're already using some form of bucket planning, I am confident that by accessing that resource you will learn new tips and techniques for getting more prospective clients to agree to move forward with you.

I'll describe why taxes are your single biggest differentiator. We didn't double down on taxes at my firm—we tripled down on them. And it starts with understanding the importance of integrating tax planning, tax management, and tax preparation into your practice. You'll have access to visuals to help you explain this to your prospects and clients. I'll share details on our marketing plan and strategy that helped us bring in over $130 million in new assets in 2023. The marketing plan keeps you focused and prevents you from chasing after the next shiny marketing object.

And you'll see the advisor career path process that has allowed me and many other elite advisors around the country to effectively multiply our capabilities as rainmakers and set up our practices to succeed far into the future.

At the end of Part II is a **Challenges and Priorities Ranking Worksheet** you can fill out to zoom in on exactly what you should focus on in your practice *right now* to jump-start growth and sustainability.

(Now, I know some of you are tempted to skip Part I and leap straight to all those resource links and the worksheet right now. If that's your inclination, go for it! I know it's hard for us entrepreneurs to follow the rules. Besides, this is meant to be an interactive book, so I invite you to navigate the chapters ahead and access the online resources in any way that makes sense to you.)

And finally in Part III—with the results of your Challenges and Priorities Ranking Worksheet firmly in hand—you'll be able to "choose your own adventure" and explore a treasure trove of additional resources for bringing more growth, professionalism, and revenue to your firm—resources for fine-tuning your holistic planning process, managing your practice more efficiently, doing cost-effective marketing, and accessing additional profitable business lines. Developed in tandem with some of the most successful financial services experts, tax professionals, and law firms in the industry, these time-tested processes will propel you forward in a systematic way that has been proven to work in practices just like yours, over and over again. You'll even get links to download some free tools you can begin using today. At the end of all that, I'll provide a list of excellent resources for further study. Essentially, you're going to be creating your own ending to this book.

So, let's seize the day and get started on your Rainmaker Multiplier journey. *Carpe diem!*

PART I

The True Story

CHAPTER 1

A Rainmaker in the Making

THE FOUNDATION

Whenever I'm asked how long I've been in the financial services field, I always say that I've been in it from the day I was born. My father started in the insurance business in the early 1970s, growing his own thriving agency in the Cleveland area where he and his thirty-five agents worked primarily in Medicare supplements, long-term care, and fixed annuities. Dad was always drumming up some crazy new idea to grow the business, so almost every night of the week we'd have an insurance agent, stockbroker, or entrepreneur over for dinner. Entrepreneurship and moneymaking ideas were always the topics of the adults' mealtime conversations. At the time I didn't think I was paying attention—I had other things on my mind like playing basketball and football and exploring the river and the woods that ran through my parents' property, and in the early years doing my best Bruce Lee impression around the neighborhood wearing the little black ninja suit I'd begged my parents to buy me. So while it might not have seemed at the time like I was absorbing the business chatter at our dinner table, now I know that I *was*. Business was the background music on the soundtrack of my childhood . . . always there, like a low hum.

THE SPARK

My first entrepreneurial adventure began when I was ten. Every Monday my dad's insurance agents would bring to the office all the checks and paperwork they'd accumulated throughout the previous week and turn them in to be processed. They would stream in all day long, and in many cases this activity would take each of them several hours to complete. So, every Monday during summer vacation, my cousin Kristy and I would set up in the parking lot of Dad's building and offer a car wash and interior detailing to the agents for five dollars a pop. Five dollars was a lot of money to a ten-year-old back then, but in hindsight it wasn't nearly enough for a full car detailing that would probably cost a couple hundred bucks today. To make matters worse, the cars were always filthy. These guys and gals practically lived out of their vehicles, and almost all of them chain-smoked (think 1980s). Cigarette butts, ashes, half-empty Big Mac containers . . . it was nasty. But Kristy and I did the work and raked in the money, and I learned a thing or two about the satisfaction of a job well done and the good things that come from treating my customers well.

Now, imagine if your dad came to you on your thirteenth birthday with a game he'd created where you would research the stock market every week for thirteen weeks and then pick a set of stocks you thought would go up. If your predictions were correct and your stocks showed gains at the end of the week, you'd win one hundred dollars. But if the stocks you chose were down, you would lose one hundred dollars. Well, that's what my dad did for me. Long story short, I ended up winning twelve out of the thirteen weeks. I now realize that this was pure luck because, as we all know, crystal balls don't exist. Regardless, I got hooked on the stock market at that young age, and my interest in business caught fire. By my senior year in high school, I knew without a doubt that I wanted to make a career in the financial services industry. Maybe as a stockbroker . . . I wasn't yet sure. The only thing I knew for certain was that I didn't want to be an insurance agent.

I played forward on my high school basketball team and was good enough that I received some offers to play college ball, but my senior year I blew out my ankle and lost all those opportunities. After I recovered, I enrolled at Cleveland State University with the goal of walking on the basketball team, but I blew out my ankle again. I was so upset—basketball had been my whole life—so after only two days in college I just said forget it, I'm going to go work for my dad.

And that's how I ended up doing the one thing I swore I'd never do: selling insurance.

KNOCK, KNOCK . . .

By the time I joined the agency, Dad was itching to retire. He'd tried numerous times to pass the agency on to one of my many siblings (I'm the youngest of eleven), but for one reason or another it never worked out. When I joined the agency, he was in the process of turning it over to my uncle, who was thrilled that he was finally getting his shot at running the business. And then I came along full of piss and vinegar and rocking the boat big time. It was my intention to take over the world, and this rubbed my uncle the wrong way.

Maybe he was threatened by me or maybe I was just causing too much disarray . . . but whatever the reason, my dad didn't have the patience to deal with it. His solution was to fire me and tell me to go start my own agency.

I began selling long-term care policies and Medicare supplements door-to-door. The work was tough, beyond brutal. I bought a stack of what they called "white cards" with the name, date of birth, and address of people who were turning sixty-five, and I would hit the streets cold calling, knocking on the doors of unsuspecting prospects.

"Hi, I'm here to see you about your insurance," I'd say.

"What insurance?" they'd say.

"Your medical insurance. Do you have a moment? I'd like to come in and do a review—"

Nine out of ten people would slam the door in my face at that point.

When somebody was kind enough to let me in, I'd ask to see their insurance card. I'd then ask to borrow their phone (this was in the Dark Ages before cell phones), and I would call the 800 number on their card and learn their benefits. After hanging up, I'd educate the person on what they had, pointing out that they lacked long-term care coverage and in most cases weren't going to have a Medicare supplement when they turned sixty-five. That's when the vast majority showed me the door. Only one in five bought a policy from me.

This was the hardest, most miserable job I've ever had to do. Most nights I went home wanting to cry. It was just constant rejection. I hated it, but I appreciate it now. It gave me a thick skin and also taught me a lot about perseverance. Basketball did that too, because it was difficult and required dedication, hard work, development of skills, constant practice, and improvement—so many skills that are directly applicable in business, skills you don't always learn in school.

A PLOT TWIST

For many years, my lack of a college degree was a sore spot for me, but now I'm actually proud of the way my career has unfolded. I'm from the school of hard knocks (literally and figuratively . . . like I said, I started out knocking on doors). I learned by doing, and I self-educated by attending every conference, reading every book, and taking every course I could get my hands on. I have to credit my dad with teaching me some of my most important lessons. He gave me a lot of great advice over the years, but there was one thing he told me early on that really shaped my philosophy: *Always do what's in the best interest of the client. If you do what's right for the client, the money will follow.*

So, while most young financial services professionals were concentrating on only one segment of the industry—either taxes, insurance, investments, or estate planning—I was determined to learn everything I could about all the different aspects of financial services. At times I focused more on the insurance side, at other times more on the investment side. For a while I dedicated myself to understanding estate planning. I earned the Certified Estate Planner designation and started working closely with a law firm that was having me do the insurance business for their clients. Things were going really well for me. I was earning over $500,000 a year and I hadn't even had my thirtieth birthday yet. I had a beautiful wife and daughter. I was feeling pretty darn good about myself.

Then, one day in 2005, I came home from the gym and didn't feel right. My heart was pounding hard and skipping beats. Clearly, something was wrong. I went to the emergency room and was diagnosed with a heart condition. There I was, only twenty-nine years old, and it hit me like a ton of bricks that I was the classic example of the shoemaker's kid . . . *the son of the insurance man had no life insurance.*

And not only that, now I would never be able to get life insurance because of my preexisting condition. I also realized that if something were to happen to me, my wife and daughter would be in a bad place because I didn't really have a business either, not in the conventional sense. My income was strictly commission based. I worked out of a storefront and had a part-time assistant. I wasn't a business owner. I was just a really good salesperson in the financial services industry. If I died, my income would die with me. You can imagine how I felt. Imagine how you would feel . . .

THE BEST ADVICE EVER

At that point I decided to dedicate myself to building a real business that would run with or without me, a business that would provide security for my family if something were to happen to me. I joined the Million Dollar Round Table Top of the Table, a worldwide organization that's all about education and growth and trying to become not only a better advisor and businessperson, but a better person all around. You had to make a minimum of $500,000 a year in commissions or fees to join, and I just barely qualified. At twenty-nine, I was one of the youngest people in the organization.

There were hundreds of financial services professionals at the first MDRT Top of the Table meeting I attended in 2006. It was very exciting. I went around and interviewed every person I could get my hands on because I wanted to find out what made these guys and gals tick, what made them so prosperous. I asked each one the same question: *To what do you attribute your career success?* Over and over again, I heard two things: join Strategic Coach—a coaching program for entrepreneurs—and charge fees for comprehensive (holistic) planning.

By the third day of the meeting, I'd lost track of who I'd already spoken to and accidentally tried to re-interview one particular man.

"Jason, do you have your wallet on you?" he asked in exasperation.

"Of course. Why?"

He grabbed me by the shoulders and spun me around so I was facing the booth Strategic Coach had set up in the meeting hall.

"Go over to that booth, pull out your wallet, give them your credit card, and tell them you want to sign up."

I guess there's no turning back now, I thought. I went to the booth, handed over my card, and joined Strategic Coach on the spot. It turned out to be one of the best decisions I've ever made (with the exception of marrying my wife, Holly). One of the main principles the program teaches is how to monetize your intellectual capital and package it into something they call a "unique process." Through that unique process I would be able to figure out a way to charge clients planning fees for the valuable advice I was giving them instead of relying solely on the products I sold them, which were primarily life insurance and annuities at that time. This was also my opportunity to start building up my own book of assets under management, because Tony DePalma, the stockbroker I had always worked with closely who handled the investments side of the business, was nearing retirement. I would now have the chance to manage the whole book of business.

This was exactly what I was looking for: the foundation for building a holistic planning practice that would run profitably and take care of my wife and daughter if, God forbid, I wasn't able to continue on. To say that I was both excited and grateful to have found a way to take control of my family's destiny would be an understatement. Once again I have to say thank you to Dan Sullivan and Strategic Coach for setting me on the path I'm about to describe to you.

CHAPTER 2

My "Unique Process"

K.I.S.S. (KEEP IT SIMPLE, SOLDIER)

One of the first things Dan Sullivan's organization, Strategic Coach, did was take me through an exercise to break down the way I served my clients into steps, and then to name those steps. As I did that, the unique process for serving my clients started to develop right before my eyes like a Polaroid picture. I then pledged to make the transformation from selling products (insurance and investments) to selling my process, with the idea that my process would sell my products for me.

> ### MY SIMPLE FOUR-STEP PROCESS
>
> 1. Discover
> 2. Design
> 3. Deliver
> 4. Dedicate

This was a major evolution for me because it put me in the light of a financial *planner* instead of a financial services professional selling products. That was a big transition because up to that point many people viewed me as a salesperson offering life insurance and annuities, but I was now getting in position to sell **a plan**—an end result for the client—their customized road map for financial security and peace of mind. Making this transition would instantly elevate my credibility. The days of only single transactions in my role as an insurance professional were over. Instead, the clients and I would be sitting on the same side of the table in an educational partnership that they would deeply appreciate and eagerly pay to continue year after year.

I remember sitting in my Strategic Coach class one day thinking about what I might call this four-step process I was devising. My coach, Kim Butler, had a company called Partners for Prosperity, and I really liked that word *prosperity*. I had also latched onto the word *clarity* because that's what I always told my clients I would bring to them if they worked with me. So there I was, brainstorming, writing out different combinations of those two words, when I jotted down the phrase *Clarity to Prosperity*. I liked it. I showed it to one of my buddies in the class.

"Hey, why don't you replace the T-O between *Clarity* and *Prosperity* with a number two?" he said. "I think that would look really cool."

I wrote it down as he suggested and instantly knew that this was it. *Clarity 2 Prosperity*, my simple four-step process for helping my clients achieve financial security and peace of mind, was officially christened.

A GAME-CHANGING DISCOVERY

Documenting and formalizing my process helped me identify strengths and weaknesses in my delivery and client interactions. For example, in the early days of my career I didn't have many visuals or props to give my clients explaining what we were going to be doing together or how the services I was offering would solve their problems. I just talked to them and sketched random concepts on a notepad. But as I started thinking deeply about how to package this process of mine, I had an epiphany that led to the identification and further development of three game-changing tools: (1) a color-coded three-ring binder organizing all of the client's financial information, (2) a visual representation of the client's customized holistic financial plan, and (3) a document depicting my four-step process and my menu of services.

The binder idea was an offshoot of something I discovered early in my career. When I started selling long-term health policies and Medicare supplements door-to-door, I was taught that the goal was "the one-appointment close." Go in and identify the gap—that was easy since hardly anybody had long-term care coverage in those days—and then offer the solution: a long-term health-care policy. But I soon realized that I had better results when I didn't rush the close—when I went in and gathered the data, told the prospect that I would go back to the office to do some homework, and returned a few days later with a solution just for them. The more I used this two-appointment approach, the more I saw a marked increase in sales and way fewer cancellations. The act of sitting down and fact-finding with the prospective client, going away to think about their situation and prepare a recommendation, and then bringing it to them at a second appointment had the effect of proving that I was willing to work for them, not just sell them a canned solution.

Later, when I started selling annuities and life insurance to my clients, I noticed that typically one spouse handled all of the couple's affairs and the other spouse had little to no idea what was going on. When the financially savvier spouse passed away, the survivor was often left in a bad situation because they didn't understand what they had and how it all worked. Clearly there was a gap that I could fill—I could sit down with couples and collaboratively gather and organize all of their financial information in one easily accessible place so that when one of them passed, the other would have all the latest data right at their fingertips. As we carried out this compiling and organizing exercise, I could educate both of them on what they currently had or didn't have, including the risk they were taking, fees they were paying, and how I might be able to develop solutions to improve their situation.

OUTFITTING MY TOOL KIT

This fact-finding and educational procedure birthed a three-ring color-coded binder containing all the client's financial, tax, and legal documents—a binder they could take home with them and that we would update every year. Following the lead of my brother Jerry, who had gathered all of these documents for his family, I created a sample binder that I could show prospective clients to pique their interest in my process. Eventually I named it the Family Estate Organizer™,[2] and my clients loved it.

---

2   For more information about the Family Estate Organizer and a free tool, see page 86.

Images 2.1: Family Estate Organizer

I even came up with a script to make sure I said the same thing to each couple every time so I didn't leave out any important points. Here's an abbreviated summary of the script:

> "Is there one of you that handles all the financial, legal, and tax affairs and knows exactly where everything is?"
>
> <wait for client to answer>
>
> Ask the one who is NOT the one who knows:
>
> "God forbid, if anything were to happen to <other

client's first name>, would you be able to take over the finances without skipping a beat?

"This binder will represent one simplified and organized place for you and your family to always know where all of your important documents are. This binder should be kept in a safe place—we recommend a fireproof safe. In our next meeting, we will organize all of your documents.

"The binder will serve a few purposes: (1) It will give the two of you a mutual filing system. When one of you passes away, the other will know exactly where everything is and how to go about your business. (2) When the second person passes away, your beneficiaries won't have to look through every file cabinet, drawer, and safety deposit box to find everything. They can settle your entire estate out of this binder. We put a checklist in here, which is called the Survivors Checklist. It tells your beneficiaries what to do Day 1, Week 1, After 1 Month, and After 6 Months, to settle your estate. (3) We will create an asset sheet[3] from everything we put in this binder. Each time we meet, we will update your asset sheet to track and monitor your progress, cash flow, and the growth of your money. (4) We will also ensure that all of your beneficiary forms and accounts are titled properly to avoid probate. Immediately after your passing, when your loved ones are

---

3   Some financial institutions do not allow the use of an asset sheet. Please check with your compliance department before discussing this point with clients.

struggling the most, they will be able to turn to us to assist them in their time of need instead of having to run to various insurance agents, tax professionals, attorneys, and other financial advisors."

This script and the sample binder were incredibly powerful tools. I saw a huge uptick in the number of prospects who decided to move forward with me once I started using them, and I retained more assets upon the original clients' passing.

A PICTURE IS WORTH A THOUSAND WORDS

The next important prop I created was the simple visual representation of the client's customized holistic financial plan. I had always explained my plans to my clients using a notepad or a dry erase board. I would draw three boxes and label them *Now, Soon,* and *Later* to represent the money they would need to have accessible to them at each of those three stages of life. I would document the balances of each account, tally up how much they currently had, and distribute that among the three boxes, writing the total above each box and circling those totals. Then I'd counsel them on the financial products or portfolios that would best meet their needs in the Now, Soon, and Later time frames and fill in any gaps. I was doing this with a client one afternoon when he pointed to the boxes and the circled dollar amounts and said, "Those look like buckets."

"Yes, they do," I replied. "I hadn't noticed that before."

"Well, I've always had a bucket *list*, and now I have a bucket *plan!*" he quipped.

This stopped me in my tracks. *The Bucket Plan!* It was the ideal visual concept for a complex financial plan of time-segmenting clients' money based on the purpose and the time horizon of when they would need it. It was simple. It was memorable. It was perfect.

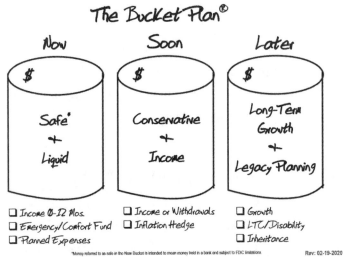

Image 2.2: The Bucket Plan

Ultimately I trademarked The Bucket Plan and began designing accompanying tools, concepts, and other visual materials I could use to simplify the delivery.[4]

Documenting my process into the four steps—Discover, Design, Deliver, and Dedicate—led me to create yet another prop I could use to show what I was going to do for prospective clients. I designed a two-sided laminated document with the four steps depicted on one side and a visual to explain the outcomes they would receive from going through the holistic wealth management process. I put

---

4   For lots more on The Bucket Plan, see page 84 in Part II and also page 116 in Part III.

this document in my desk drawer so it would be handy during client meetings. During our first meeting I would ask the clients "discovery" questions, including having them rank their most pressing priorities or concerns regarding their current financial situation. Once we'd identified their biggest fears or concerns, I could whip out the laminated document[5] and show them how I offered the exact services that would address their top concerns or priorities, along with the process we would follow for getting it done now and continuing into the future as their needs changed.

The Bucket Plan®
Holistic Planning in Your Best Interest

1 Discover
Where You Are Now

- About You
- Your Goals & Objectives
- Your Current Finances & Taxes
- Your Priorities
- Our Services
- The Process

2 Design
Where You Want To Go

- Organizing Your Financial Life
- Understanding Your Net Worth
- Assessing Your Cash Flow
- Tax Return Review
- Analyzing Your Risk
- Developing Your Plan

3 Deliver
Your Holistic Plan

- Finalize Your Customized Bucket Plan
- Align Investments with Your Market Volatility Tolerance
- Optimize Your Cash Flow
- Provide Solutions
- Transition Plan & Implementation

4 Dedicated
Service and Support

- Active Plan Management
- Ongoing Advice
- Tax & Wealth Management
- Proactive Communication & Education
- Plan Update Meetings

Image 2.3: The Bucket Plan List

---

5   Learn more about this document on pages 85 and 86.

Prepared for: _____ Date: _____	Deliverables
Retirement Income Distribution Plan	
Goals Based Financial Plan	
Volatility Tolerance & Investment Alignment	
Periodic Review Meeting	
Proactive Wealth Management	
Cash Flow Assessment	
Social Security Optimization	
Pension Maximization	
401(k) and Qualified Plan Allocation Analysis	
Investment Audit	
General Financial Advice	
Financial Modeling Report	
Medical / Medicare[1] Insurance Evaluation	
Long Term Care / Disability Risk Mitigation	
Life Insurance Audit / Needs Analysis	
Charitable Giving Strategies	
The Family Estate Organizer	
Beneficiary Designation Review & Update	
The Family Succession Plan	
Estate Planning Document Review[2]	
Estate Tax Reduction	
Probate Avoidance Strategies	
Annual Tax Loss / Gain Harvesting	
Roth Conversion Bracket Bumping	
Prior Year Tax Return Review	
Income Tax Reduction Strategies	
Your Customized Bucket Plan	

[1]For Clients 65 and older
[2]Legal document review provided by independent counsel; update to documents may require additional fee.

Cost: $ REV. 12-06-2021

Image 2.4: Deliverables

Showing these visuals and point-of-sale materials to my clients took a complex and intangible concept—financial planning—and turned it into a tangible one. Being able to show them the philosophy of bucketing and the process they would be going through—showing them what they would be paying me for and the ongoing services they would receive—was an enormous breakthrough. It grew my practice tremendously, not only because it served the clients better, but also because it gave them the ability to explain my process to others. They could easily articulate what I did for them and even tell their friends and loved ones about their Family Estate Organizer™ and their Bucket Plan. It gave them a more concise way to refer people to me. I saw an increase in referrals and an increase in my capability to get paid for the process I was taking people through rather than just getting paid for the solutions I was recommending.

The system also codified and streamlined everything for my support staff. The process and deliverables offered a road map my team could follow to help all of us serve our clients better. Training new employees was easier because our process was systematized. We would no longer be winging it. We were on our way to becoming a well-oiled machine. I was beginning to see how this thing could truly turn my practice into a sustainable business that could run with or without me, which was my ultimate goal. Duplicatable, scalable, repeatable—that was what I wanted, and I had a good feeling that this process might get me there. All that was left was to keep using it and tweaking it, over and over again, to see how it worked in real life.

A MEMORABLE TEST CASE

All my clients are important to me, but my meeting with one particular couple—"Jerry and Irene"[6]—stands out as one of the most meaningful interactions of my career because they showed me that this process I'd cooked up might actually be something special.

Jerry was one of our community's most respected commercial construction managers. At the time we met, he had recently scaled back his work and was doing some part-time consulting with the goal of retiring in the next two years. Jerry was very excited about his upcoming retirement and wanted to make sure everything was in order so that he and his wife, Irene, a semiretired teacher, wouldn't have to bother with any financial hassles in their later years. When

---

6   Their real names and other identifying information have been altered to protect their privacy.

he called to make the appointment for our initial consultation, he said to me, "Jason, you and I can just take care of this ourselves. I've always been the one to handle our finances. I'm not sure Irene would even be interested."

While I respected Jerry's desire to spare his wife the details of hammering out a financial plan, I insisted that she be involved from the start. I explained that if anything were to happen to one of them, the survivor would need to understand the reality of what was going on with their finances. I told him that I take my clients through a comprehensive learning process as we prepare their plans, and I wanted both of them to receive all the benefits of that education. Once I explained it that way, Jerry agreed with my rationale and Irene participated in every meeting from then on. To Jerry's delight, Irene turned out to be keenly interested in learning about their financial situation. She thoroughly enjoyed our meetings and had a great time offering her input and asking questions.

As part of the educational process and the creation of Jerry and Irene's comprehensive financial plan, I used The Bucket Plan planning process to fact-find, analyze, and advise them on their entire financial situation: investments, insurance, taxes, Social Security, health care, and estate planning for when one or both of them passed away. To kick things off, we started by engaging in a discovery conversation about their top priorities, goals, and concerns in retirement. We needed to understand them and their family history in order to customize their plan based on *their* priorities, not anyone else's. Next we gathered information about all of their assets and income sources. We then used an assessment tool we had developed to determine if there was going to be a gap between the amount of money they'd need for day-to-day living during their first decade of retirement versus the income they'd be receiving each month from Social Security and pensions. We also conducted an analysis to determine their tolerance for market volatility and risk in each bucket separately (yet another tool we developed as part of the four-step process). Once we'd collected all this data and information, we used it to strategically allocate their assets in accordance with The Bucket Plan philosophy, giving them confidence and peace of mind while simultaneously helping them achieve their goals and expectations for growth going forward.

I LOVE IT WHEN A PLAN COMES TOGETHER

Among other things, we put in place a life insurance policy that would pay off Jerry and Irene's mortgage and give some additional liquidity and income replacement to the surviving spouse when the first one passed away. We calculated their future tax liability and made sure we had money in place to cover all the bases, so there would be no unpleasant income tax bill from the IRS down the road. We ensured that all their assets were correctly titled and their beneficiaries were properly designated so they wouldn't accidently disinherit any of their loved ones. By doing so, Jerry and Irene felt confident their survivors would be spared the cost and burden of having to settle their estate in probate court. And we had all their important financial information gathered together logically into the Family Estate Organizer (the three-ring binder I'd developed) so everything would be accessible at a moment's notice whenever Jerry and Irene needed it.

Unfortunately, Irene would need it sooner rather than later. Within a year of putting together their Bucket Plan, Jerry was killed in a horrific car accident. Irene was suddenly a widow. She was devastated, as was everyone in the community who knew Jerry. He was such a great guy.

A few days after Jerry's funeral, Irene and I met in my office. She was still in shock about the heartbreaking turn her life had taken. I settled her into a chair in my office, took out a marker and her Bucket Plan documents, and began laying everything out for her on the big whiteboard on the wall. I drew the three buckets—a "Now" bucket, a "Soon" bucket, and a "Later" bucket. I showed her how the life insurance policy we'd put in place for Jerry was going to pay off her mortgage completely. I showed her how the money we'd put into her Now bucket was going to give her sufficient funds for emergencies or anything else unexpected that might crop up in the near future. I showed her how the Soon bucket we'd set up was going to supply the next ten years' worth of income. Then I sketched out how the Later bucket we'd established would give her growth and an income for the rest of her life beyond the next ten years, plus an ample number of other investments to outpace inflation. In short, I showed her that the holistic plan we had produced would completely fill all the financial gaps created by Jerry's untimely death.

I finished my overview and turned to face Irene. She sat in dead silence looking down at the conference table for what seemed like an eternity. At last she looked up at me with tears rolling down her face and said with a decisive nod, "Jason, I'm going to be okay, aren't I?"

"Yes, Irene," I replied. "You are going to be okay. And I'm going to be right here to help you stay that way."

With that she stood up, walked over, and gave me the biggest hug I've ever had in my life. Irene's a small lady, but that hug had tremendous power behind it. I must admit that I teared up too. What an incredible feeling to know that the process I'd worked so hard to develop had helped Irene gain some measure of peace during her darkest hour. And what an incredible feeling for Irene to realize that she had the knowledge and the financial plan to live out the rest of her life in comfort.

A BROADENING FOCUS

At that point I knew that this process was good. *Really* good. It allowed me to offer the sort of elite services usually reserved for ultra-high-net-worth clients, to middle-class millionaires like Jerry and Irene. The process worked, not only for clients like Irene but also for me and my team. This inspired me to write a book called *The Bucket Plan: Protecting and Growing Your Assets for a Worry-Free Retirement*, which ended up getting more attention than I ever thought it would—including being named by *U.S. News & World Report* as one of the Top 10 Retirement Planning Books in 2023! It's the only book on that list about the retirement planning process as a whole.

Image 2.5: *The Bucket Plan* Book Accolades

I love this industry. I want other advisors to be successful professionals because the more of us there are, the better it is for everyone. You know how the "rising tide lifts all boats"—the more advisors who know these concepts, the more we can help people and maximize our reach as an industry. I know that the vast majority of us want to do this work correctly. We never want to harm our clients in any way. But I also know that good intentions are not enough. By operating as transactional salespeople, advisors run the risk of shirking their fiduciary duty. This comprehensive process of The Bucket Plan, on the other hand, could help them evolve into valued partners and trusted allies for every person who might come to them for financial guidance and help.

Because of my heart condition, I had to go to the doctor's office on a regular basis for several years so they could monitor my situation. I was sitting in my doctor's waiting room for one of those checkups not long after Jerry passed when it dawned on me how similar a health-care setting is to a holistic wealth management practice. There is a lot at stake in both settings, but there's one big difference: The medical profession has clear policies and procedures for every patient interaction. Doctors and nurses must follow a strict protocol for communicating with patients, a protocol that includes asking a series of critical questions, explaining potential outcomes, and formally discussing the risks and side effects for every procedure, every medication, and every therapy recommendation. For each decision the doctor and patient must make along the course of treatment, there is an educational conversation and a corresponding form or waiver. It's all about education, documentation, full disclosure, and achieving a meeting of the minds.

Health-care professionals and hospitals don't operate this way because it's fun. They do it to protect themselves and to educate their patients. It is just as critical in our profession to ensure that everyone is on the same page, and this model could help make that happen every single time for every single client . . . but only if other advisors will adopt and implement it.

LET'S RAISE THIS BABY TOGETHER, TOO!

Right after my heart diagnosis—when I realized I had to create my own life insurance to take care of Holly and our one daughter at the time, Jordan, if I were suddenly gone—Holly joined me to help build JL Smith into a self-sustaining company that could produce cash flow with or without me. She'd had a successful nine-year career at the Social Security Administration up to that point, but we both knew her talents would be better utilized in making JL Smith as successful as we knew it could and needed it to be. Holly and I were such a great team at home raising Jordan that we figured we could also be a great team at work raising this business. Her arrival on the scene was a game changer for the company. The organization and structure she was able to provide took us to another level, freeing me up to allocate time and effort to studying the game of business and learning how to build a company that would thrive far into the future.

As I write this, I'm thinking about my current five kids and various businesses, and the similarities between raising successful children and raising a successful business. Both need love, sacrifice, structure, and care. Both require a tremendous amount of hard work, patience, and discipline. If you don't do all these things the right way, the kids/business might turn out wrong, and that would be heartbreaking because of all the time and effort you put in.

I've been blessed to have all my businesses and kids turn out pretty well (so far), but the process never really ends, because no matter how old they get, they are always going to be your baby.

A NEW (OLD) HOME FOR MY PRACTICE

As if I didn't have enough going on, I decided around this same time to move out of my storefront office into a new space, one that better reflected the elite level of service I was providing my clients. I had attended an MDRT Top of the Table conference where I was fortunate to hear a speaker talk about his experience renovating a historic home and turning it into his financial services office. He described the many benefits of operating in a unique environment like this and the culture that naturally sprang from working within it—the welcoming feeling it created among the team and clients. He said that clients were raving about how much they loved coming to an office that felt so warm and familiar, like the home in which they'd grown up. This got my attention because I wished to create a unique environment for my practice too, but I hadn't been able to articulate exactly what I wanted to do. Now I knew. I was going to follow that guy's lead and look for my own historic home to renovate and turn into an office for JL Smith.

Holly and I were big fans of fixer-upper shows on HGTV, so when I told her about my idea, she was up for the challenge. We soon found what looked like the perfect place—an abandoned house in the heart of the Avon Historical District. This house was in bad shape. The roof was leaking. Vines were growing up the exterior siding and in through the windows. Creaky floors, holes in the walls, faulty electrical and plumbing—it was a mess. But it was *our* mess. We loved it from the moment we walked in the door.

Image 2.6: The Office Before Renovation

Image 2.7: The Office After Renovation

We bought it and launched into our own personal version of *This Old House*. During the day I made house calls to my clients and spent evenings and weekends renovating the property. We had lots of friends, family, staff, and even clients pitch in to help us along the way. One of my closest friends and my largest client at the time was the late Herb Brew of Herb's Tavern in Rocky River, creator of the famous Herb Burger. He had been a plumber before opening his restaurant, and he did all the plumbing for us. My cousin

Jimbo did the drywalling. My sister Sharon and brother-in-law Randy helped me with the painting. A client who was a cabinet-maker constructed the built-ins and conference tables. It truly was a family-and-friends undertaking. By the time we'd finished, the love that had gone into salvaging that home was palpable. Our clients told us over and over again how beautiful the office was and how much they enjoyed visiting it. The house was a wonderful investment that has paid great dividends.

ASSEMBLING THE DREAM TEAM

A couple of years after the house was done, we decided to launch a new education training company called Clarity 2 Prosperity (C2P). Through this company we would teach the four-step holistic planning process to advisors, which we renamed The Bucket Plan. For help with C2P, I recruited Dave Alison, my marketer at my then-current registered investment advisor (RIA) and insurance marketing organization (IMO). The moment I met Dave I could see the brilliance in him; he was something really special. He was very young—I think around twenty-four years old at the time—and I saw unlimited upside potential to having him join me. I considered him to be the perfect person to help me with C2P and simultaneously spark up an RIA and an IMO. Only challenge was, I would have to convince him to leave the sun-drenched beaches of Tampa, Florida, where he was living at the time, and return to his hometown of Cleveland—in the winter, no less! Not only that, he'd be moving into the dark, musty basement of my house with our fish, Sam, and sleeping on a pull-out sofa while we got C2P up and running. I knew it would cost a lot financially to launch these companies, so this was the best I could offer him. Despite all that, Dave said yes. Talk about commitment and dedication to the vision. I tapped my old friend Pablo Terra (the best man at my wedding and a whiz at identifying and developing great people) to work with Dave in the backstage.

We also brought in some of the top financial and insurance professionals with the RIA and IMO we were doing our business with, to be practicing partners: Don Chamberlin (the number-one advisor the previous year), John Del Greco (the master of referrals), and Carl Smith (a rainmaker with a presence). These guys were critical additions to our lineup. Don and Carl both had big, thriving tax practices. I didn't have one, but I wanted one for three reasons. First, it's a great way to get in front of more people. Second, in order to be a true holistic advisor, you have to put tax planning and management into your clients' financial plan, not just handle their tax prep. And third, I'd learned that the one common denominator in all the top financial planning firms was that they had some sort of a relationship with a tax practice. They'd either built one, bought one, or borrowed the services of an existing one, referring their financial services clients to the tax practice and having the tax practice refer their clients to the financial services firm. Build it, buy it, or borrow it?[7] Which would it be? All are great ways to get rolling with a tax practice, but for me it made the most sense to borrow one . . . or so I thought.

I knew only two tax professionals at the time. The first was the person who did my and my extended family's taxes. I talked to them about working with their clients, but they didn't give me any referrals or do any joint marketing. The conversation went

---

7   See page 105 in Part II and page 121 in Part III for more information about adding a tax
    practice, including access to downloadable tools.

nowhere. Then I approached the certified public accountant (CPA) who was doing the tax work for my clients. She had done a fantastic job on all the tax modeling (the "what if" scenarios, what triggers tax on Social Security, Roth conversions, what the tax liability would be if we cashed something in, and so on). I tried to "borrow it" from her, to see if she would let me work her client base. Again, dead end.

At that point I knew that if I really wanted to be able to leverage tax preparation clients to become financial clients, I'd either have to build or buy a tax practice. Truth be told, I was overwhelmed at the prospect of buying one. I didn't know how to get a loan or raise money. I knew nothing about acquisitions. For me, buying seemed so much more intimidating than building, but even building seemed like a huge undertaking. Was it even worth pursuing?

WE CAN DO THIS!

For many years I had seen firsthand how the Medicare supplement model that I had been running had helped us get in front of new financial services prospects. I would have Medicare agents sell the supplemental policy and then I'd deliver it, which was a profitable lead-generation solution for selling life insurance and annuities. When I heard of the tax prep model that Don Chamberlin and Carl Smith were running, I realized that it could do the same thing for lead generation as the Medicare supplements. We'd have our people do the tax returns, and then I could deliver the returns and talk about tax planning as it related to the clients' savings and investments.

Having a tax practice would bring so many benefits to my holistic wealth management firm. It would differentiate us from other advisors who didn't offer tax planning, management, and prep. It would help us attract that desirable mass affluent client demographic we were targeting.

Creating a systematic process for incorporating tax services into our holistic plans would allow us to scale our business and more easily train associate advisors. It would help us deliver better outcomes for our clients, including investment decisions around tax sensitive asset allocation, all while differentiating ourselves from the other financial advisors in our community. We would have a higher likelihood of helping our clients achieve their goals.

Those are just a few of the many reasons I decided to build a tax practice and why I wanted Don and Carl as my partners at C2P—I wanted to learn how to do what they were already doing so successfully. Together we set about creating all the systems to make it easier for my office and others that joined C2P to implement this model.

CASH IS KING, BUT HOLLY IS THE QUEEN

As a start-up, our overhead immediately jumped to over $100,000 a month. I continued to work seven days a week, fifteen hours a day. It was a crazy time. I didn't take a salary. I threw everything I had at my businesses, including my retirement accounts. The years of making a $500,000 salary were gone temporarily in the quest for launching the new company with a bigger potential upside.

I will never forget the day I cashed those in. I was pretty much down to zero and I decided it was time to have a sit-down with Holly and Jordan, who was fourteen at the time, and let them know where we stood financially. The three of us gathered around the kitchen table and I laid it all out for them—how I'd leveraged everything we had to the point that we might have to sell our house and move into the attic above the newly renovated office.

When Jordan heard this, she burst into tears. She was practically inconsolable.

But Holly? She didn't say a word. Didn't ask me a single question, didn't raise any objection, didn't shed a single tear. She never flinched. She just nodded in acceptance of our new and uncertain reality. I'll never forget how strong she was . . . how much she believed in me and trusted me. It was the biggest AHA! moment of my life: Holly was the best business partner of them all. Knowing that she was firmly by my side gave me the strength and resolve to keep pushing forward.

CHAPTER 3

Jeff and the Drive to Be Number One

LET'S DO LUNCH

At the same time that I started building the C2P dream team, in 2011 I was tapped to speak at an industry event about the holistic planning process and the growth JL Smith had achieved after implementing it. I was answering questions at the conclusion of the talk when a life insurance wholesaler who had waited patiently for the last people to leave walked up and introduced himself.

"You're out of Cleveland, right?" he asked as he shook my hand.

"Yes, I'm in Avon, which is part of the Cleveland metro area," I replied.

"One of my best friends from college is a fantastic financial planner who lives in Avon," he said. "His name is Jeff Warnkin. I'd love to introduce you to him because I think he could really benefit from hearing about this model of yours. Are you interested in meeting him?"

Always eager to connect with other financial planners—even my competitors—I gave this gentleman my contact information and within a few days found myself sitting across the table from Jeff Warnkin at one of my favorite lunch spots. I liked the guy immediately. He was about ten years older than me, personable, funny, and very intelligent. His dad and mine were both insurance men, so we had that in common. We found that we were also kindred spirits when it came to our love of financial services. Jeff had invested heavily in his education, earning CPA and Certified Financial Planner (CFP) designations and a master's in taxation. I was impressed, as my education had been more informal (i.e., knocking on doors selling insurance straight out of high school).

"Congratulations!" I said when he told me about his designations and expansive experience. "You must have a super successful practice."

As soon as those words came out of my mouth, Jeff's body language changed. He literally deflated a bit and sighed.

"It's going okay, I guess," he said with a shrug. "But . . ."

"But what?" I asked.

"Well, the 2008/09 financial crisis hit me and my clients really hard, and I just thought I'd be doing better by this point in my career, you know? My brother, he's also in the business and he's killing it. And back in the day my dad was number one in his company. I've never had that kind of success and I don't know why, because I have what it takes. I want to be at the top, too."

I'd seen that kind of dejection before—many times, in fact—on the faces of other seasoned financial planners who had been doing their best for their clients every day for years, sometimes decades, yet still felt like they were spinning their wheels . . . missing the mark . . . leaving too much money on the table.

I asked Jeff a few questions about how he ran his practice and delivered products and services to his clients, and it became clear pretty quickly that his practice lacked processes and structure. As he explained it, he was having to walk alongside anyone he hired and hold their hands, step-by-step every day, and show them how to best support him with each new client, each new prospect, each service/product delivery.

"Frankly, it's just easier to do it all myself," he said. "I'm a really good financial planner, but I'm lousy at managing a team. Not good at marketing either, by the way. I'm in my midforties, Jason. If I haven't conquered this by now, I wonder if I ever will."

"Okay, let me stop you right there," I said. "I'm going to give you the key to the whole thing in just one sentence."

Jeff chuckled with an expression of skepticism. "The whole thing in one sentence, eh? This I gotta hear . . ."

A LESSON FROM STARBUCKS

"Okay, here it is," I said. "The key, Jeff, is that *you have to systematize what you're doing in the front stage with the clients, and then have the backstage supporting you such that the process is seamless and is the same every time.* That's the only way your staff will know how to help you so you can then devote your time to getting in front of new people and being the rock star financial planner that you are."

Jeff nodded thoughtfully as I continued.

"But first you've got to be running a succinct process so everybody in your office will know what to do . . . step-by-step, exactly what's going to happen every time. Of course, you're always going to customize each client's plan, but the steps you and your people follow as you put those custom plans together have got to be the same every time if you want to build a thriving practice that can run with or without you."

I offered Jeff the example of the process Starbucks uses for serving coffee to their customers.

"You go into Starbucks and they take your order," I said. "They will customize your drink however you tell them to . . . whether you want soy milk, almond milk, an extra shot of espresso, whatever you want is fine. The barista asks your name, you pay them, and they send you to wait at the end of the counter. You know that a few minutes later they're going to call your name and you'll pick up your drink and it will be in the same kind of cup with the same kind of lid as always. It's consistent, and the process of preparing and delivering it is practically automated from start to finish. Every Starbucks employee knows the system for creating custom drinks and they don't deviate from it.

"Now, compare that to your practice," I continued. "You've got all this amazing knowledge in your head—the equivalent of an excellent cup of coffee—and you know all the various ingredients you can use to make that cup perfect for each customer. You're a CFP, a CPA, a master's in taxation . . . you should be a world-class barista at delivering financial plans. But unfortunately, everyone who comes into your shop is having a different experience every time because you don't have a process for preparing and serving the plans. You're just winging it on a notepad. Your employees don't know how to help the clients or you, so you're having to divert your attention from your clients to fixing the mess going on backstage. Before you know it, balls are getting dropped and opportunities are falling through the cracks."

"Yeah, that pretty much describes my practice." Jeff chuckled. "No wonder I'm not at the top of my game."

"*Yet*," I said. "There is no reason you can't be number one, Jeff. Your entire career has brought you to this point. You just need the right processes and structure for your business, and I can help you get there. Would you like to learn how? I'd be happy to teach you."

Jeff didn't hesitate.

"I'm in," he said decisively. "How soon can we start?"

"That's the spirit! Let's set a date and dive in."

CHAPTER 4

Bryan, the Young Gun

ROUGH AROUND THE EDGES

Around the time I met Jeff, I got a phone call from an old family friend and personal stockbroker, Tony DePalma, with a proposition for me. Tony explained that his nephew, Bryan Bibbo, had just graduated from Kent State with a degree in accounting and was looking for a firm to join so he could gain some real-world experience.

"He's a really bright kid," Tony said. "He's got a good future ahead of him. He just needs some guidance, a mentor, and I thought of you. I've taught him everything I know, but the future is the holistic planning model you're running. Are you interested in taking him on?"

I was super busy getting C2P up to speed. That, coupled with my own thriving practice, kept me hopping. I wasn't sure there were enough hours in the day for me to mentor Tony's nephew and tend to all my other responsibilities. But because I respected Tony so much, I agreed to meet with Bryan to discuss the possibility.

I'll never forget the day that kid walked into my office for the interview. In fact, it still makes me laugh after all these years. Bryan was so young and unpolished . . . he had this head full of wild, untamed black hair, a crazy loud tie, baggy jacket. He almost looked like a cartoon character. And then he started talking and I got *really* concerned. Like many young Cleveland guys, Bryan was a big fan of hip-hop music and culture. He literally sounded like a rapper when he spoke, and his vocabulary was atrocious.

"Yo, Jason, thanks for meetin' me today," he said. "I'm pumped!"

Now, I grew up playing basketball on the playgrounds of some pretty rough neighborhoods outside of Cleveland. Although I shared Bryan's appreciation for hip-hop culture, I also knew that sounding like Snoop Dogg when you're trying to talk to baby boomers about their retirement nest egg wasn't going to fly. But out of loyalty to Tony, I hired Bryan as an intern at ten dollars an hour, and we set about the task of making him presentable.

"I know you're smart, Bryan," I told him, "but if you're ever going to be taken seriously in this industry, you have to look and talk more like a professional."

"Word," he replied with a solemn nod.

Man, I thought, *I love a challenge as much as the next guy, but I'm not sure it's going to be possible to whip this kid into shape!*

Yet Bryan was full of surprises. Not long after I hired him, he came to my office to tell me about a vocabulary course he'd purchased, and he promised to study it every day. True to his word, he followed through. In no time we saw an improvement in his ability to communicate more professionally. He also started doing a lot more reading. I gave him all my favorite business books, and he gobbled them up.

GRAB YOUR BOW AND ARROW, KID!

Tax season was soon upon us, and Bryan shined. The clients loved him, the staff loved him. He was just a super hardworking, personable kid. At the conclusion of tax season I offered him a full-time position at $25,000 a year. Granted, it wasn't a lot of money, but it was enough to keep him alive and give us some time to really gauge his potential. He continued to excel. Everybody was telling him that he was doing a great job, and he was thoroughly enjoying the accolades.

Six months later Bryan asked if he and I could have a talk. As he sat across from me, I marveled at how much he'd changed since the day he'd first slouched into my office looking like he'd just stumbled out of a club. Well-groomed, professionally attired, and speaking with confidence and composure, this was a more polished Bryan—one who was clearly on his right path. He took a deep breath and looked me in the eye.

"Jason, I'd like a raise," he said resolutely. "I've worked really hard, and I believe I deserve it. Twenty-five thousand is well below what my peers are making. I know I can earn more money somewhere else, but I love it here and I'd like to stay."

"You're right, you have worked hard and we'd like for you to stay too," I said. "So I'll tell you what I'm going to do, Bryan. I'm going to raise you to thirty-five thousand."

"Oh, thank you! You won't be sorry—"

"But," I interrupted, "and this is a big 'but,' so listen carefully: *This will be the last raise I'm ever going to give you.* You will never get another raise as long as you stay here."

Bryan's smile dissolved into a look of shock and confusion.

"Wait . . . what? Never another raise? You mean, *forever*?"

"Yes, that's what I mean."

"But why?"

"Because you won't need raises. I'm going to teach you how to hunt."

"Like, with a bow and arrow?"

"No," I laughed. "I mean like hunting for new clients and new opportunities on your own. I'm going to show you how to make your own pay raises, build a book of business, form alliances, lead a team. Once you've learned all that, the sky will be the limit for you. You won't need to grovel for a raise ever again. You'll be controlling your own destiny. Can you imagine how cool that will be?"

I needn't have asked that question. Bryan was grinning from ear to ear. I could practically see the gears turning in his mind as he imagined all the wonderful possibilities.

AS FATE WOULD HAVE IT

Having just read these accounts of my earliest interactions with Jeff and Bryan, you might think that our coming together was a random event, the kind of happenstance encounters that take place every day in the business world. I thought the same thing at the time. No big deal, really . . . Jeff and Bryan were nice, capable guys, and I was lending them a hand by passing on what I knew about running a holistic financial planning business.

What I didn't realize was that they were about to teach *me* a thing or two. These were not run-of-the-mill chance meetings at all. They actually represented the dawn of something big and life changing for me, because they were the catalyst for my new way of thinking about how to build and run a self-sustaining holistic wealth management practice.

CHAPTER 5

The Stress Test

HELP ME HELP YOU

Following our initial lunch meeting, Jeff and I scheduled time to spend four days together going over the elements of our holistic planning process and practice along with my new partners at C2P. From there I spent the next few months coaching him and trying to help him grow his practice. He attempted to hire an assistant and, after an intense search, got it narrowed down to two good candidates. Neither one worked out. Jeff was so frustrated. He was on the verge of throwing in the towel.

By now I knew for a fact that Jeff was a great financial and tax planner and a stand-up guy to boot. He was smart, dedicated, and a quick learner. I couldn't just let him give up. I started to think about asking him to join me at JL Smith, and the more I thought about it, the more it made sense. I needed a top-notch advisor to service my clients, and Jeff was the perfect candidate. He already had a small tax practice that he wasn't marketing or growing, whereas my tax practice was taking off. He would be a terrific asset there. I couldn't work 100 hours a week forever . . . Jeff could take over a block of my clients so I could focus on growing C2P. And by merging his practice with mine, Jeff would have the opportunity to do what he does best—be a financial planner—and not have to worry about hiring, staffing, delegating, marketing, and all the things he didn't care to do. My team would take all of that off his plate.

I became convinced that Jeff and I would be so much stronger together than we were as individuals, so I asked him if he wanted to join forces with me. Thankfully, he said yes. We merged his practice into mine, and he took over the bulk of my B- and C-list clients with Bryan's support so I could focus on the A-list while simultaneously expanding the reach of C2P.

MENTORING AND MOMENTUM

Meanwhile, Bryan was off to the races. He shadowed me, attending my meetings and watching how I interacted with clients and team members. It was fun guiding him through the earliest days of his career and watching him grow more capable and confident. However, as I got busier with C2P, I realized that I didn't have the time to mentor him from a financial advisor standpoint.

It was then that Jeff stepped in and supported our young teammate as he learned the ropes. I continued to mentor Bryan in business, entrepreneurship, leadership, and management, but Jeff taught him everything he knew about financial and tax planning. This tag team approach to guiding Bryan's development was a winning formula. With each passing day our team grew stronger and more proficient . . . and consequently, our practice started to pick up steam. I was being invited to speak at more industry events, and more advisors were joining C2P. They were either aligning with our RIA or IMO or paying a monthly fee in order to plug into The Bucket Plan process and our resources for building a holistic business model. Simultaneously we were using and refining the process in our real-world financial services lab at JL Smith. The momentum was building at C2P, and we were finally seeing it in the financials.

THE POWER OF THE PROCESS

Over the next few years, the building blocks for creating a self-sustaining holistic wealth management practice took shape. We brought on an instructional design team at C2P that specialized in transfer of knowledge and the way the adult mind learns, and documented everything in detailed processes and systems so everybody could repeat and replicate the success of JL Smith and our other partner model offices, as well as the best practices of each new partner or advisor who joined C2P. We really cracked the code for teaching people how to emulate and repeat the successes of others. As the years ticked along, we continued to refine The Bucket Plan process at JL Smith and other top-producing offices with C2P to make it even more efficient and simple. Jeff and Bryan were true believers . . . they were killing it and bringing in more revenue and referrals than ever.

I have a true story that illustrates the power of this process. Jeff and I were out of town at a Mastermind group meeting where we were teaching financial planners The Bucket Plan, the tax model, marketing tactics, and so on. One afternoon when we took a break, I saw that I'd received a voicemail from Bryan back at the office. He said that someone had walked in off the street and wanted to roll over $800,000 of investments, and they needed to do it *right away*. He had scheduled an appointment for them to return the next day, and he was calling me to find out what to do.

Bryan had just gotten his Series 65 license. He had never closed a piece of business or brought on a client before. I could hear the nervousness and excitement in his voice—this was going to be his big chance! I called him back and instructed him to go onto our e-Learning site where we had just posted the first version of The Bucket Plan process. The step-by-step module covered all the different tools and concepts, including what to say and do in the first meeting. There he could download all the forms, including the fact finder and the volatility tolerance analysis, to help him determine how much should go into each bucket.

"Bryan, you've got twenty-four hours before that client comes back," I said. "So I want you to spend those hours watching that module over and over again until you know it inside out. You've got this, okay? You can do this."

"Yes, I'm on it!" he replied.

The next day I called him back to see how the meeting had gone, and sure enough, Bryan had been able to walk the client through the process, completing all the paperwork to roll over the $800,000. He was so proud of himself.

"I watched the training like seven times last night," he said, "and by the time that client walked in, I was ready."

That's the story of Bryan's first piece of business, and it shows the power of having a process that a new advisor can plug into and use straight out of the gate.

A REALIZATION

As I watched the evolution of Bryan, Jeff, and myself and the other advisors joining the C2P family of friends, I noticed that there are **three types of advisors** who benefit the most from using The

Bucket Plan process. The first is **those who operate primarily on a transactional basis but want to transition to planning**. This could be a person who has had a lot of success at gathering assets under management (AUM) or placing insurance products, someone who's built a career on a wink and a smile, building bonds and rapport. People listen to them and trust them so much that they end up doing a transaction with them. These advisors already know where the puck is going, and they also know that they will be even more successful if they make the shift to holistic planning. The Bucket Plan fits the bill.

The next kind of advisors are **those who need to simplify their presentations so people can actually understand them** . . . advisors like Jeff who go out and earn their CFP, CPA, a master's in taxation, and every other designation they can find. They have more knowledge in their pinkie finger than most of us will ever have in our entire bodies, but at the end of the day they struggle with sales. They get a lot of "think it overs" and perplexed looks because they sometimes talk over people's heads. Again, The Bucket Plan is the solution because it simplifies the sophistication.

The final type of advisor who gravitates toward The Bucket Plan is like I was—**the solo rainmaker with no succession plan**. When they die, their practice dies with them . . . or it becomes a fire sale for their spouse to deal with. Everybody suffers, including the clients who are left in the lurch. The Bucket Plan resolves this by letting solo practitioners and the advisors they bring on plug into a system that's scalable and duplicatable so they can grow their practice for the future. Recall how Bryan was when he first joined our practice. At first we had him doing tax prep and Medicare supplements as a way to cut his teeth on working with clients. People loved him. He was truly great at sales and service, but he didn't yet know how to do financial planning. He needed a process to guide him as he learned. The Bucket Plan was a crucial part of the answer.

Jeff, Bryan, and the scores of other advisors who had joined C2P were using The Bucket Plan to help them overcome their challenges and build on their strengths. Watching all of them grow in their success was so fulfilling. I was growing too. For me, there's nothing more rewarding than playing a role in other people's success. Luckily, Jeff and Bryan provided me with that opportunity and led me to some interesting epiphanies about how to develop my practice even further.

FARMERS AND HUNTERS

The more I got to know Jeff and Bryan, the more I saw how their different personalities affected their work. Jeff was great at service delivery and taking care of the clients. He really cared about them, and it showed. He tended them like plants in a garden, nurturing them and making sure they were thriving. His rationale was that if they were happy, they would become loyalists. They'd keep coming back to him for more, and they'd refer their family and friends, too. I started thinking of Jeff as equivalent to a *farmer*, one who sticks close to home and cultivates relationships that will bring him new opportunities.

Bryan, on the other hand, had the temperament of a *hunter*—one who goes out into the wilderness, identifies and seizes opportunities, kills them, drags them home, and shares them with the rest of the village. Outgoing and fantastic at making connections, people like Bryan—with their direct, take-charge nature and their innate sense of urgency—might not have the patience (initially) to tend and nurture the crop slowly and steadily like a farmer, but they're awesome at developing new opportunities and getting people to take action.

Both Jeff and Bryan were great with clients but with different strengths. Ideally, both of them would learn how to become proficient at farming *and* hunting. Because of Jeff's keen focus on nurturing existing client relationships, he would need encouragement and pushing in order to learn business development (hunting skills). And because of the way Bryan was hardwired, he would get bored and frustrated if he were stuck farming all the time. Quality control in the front stage is everything. Bryan would need time in the backstage to learn the finer points of service delivery before we turned him loose . . . but turning him loose was the ultimate goal.

LADDERS AND CHAIRS

As I thought about these two men and how they fit into our practice, I realized how important it is to do your due diligence to make sure you're not accidently hiring someone who's great at farming when what you really wanted was someone who's great at hunting, or vice versa. While I firmly believe that people can learn and evolve, a leader has to understand what makes people tick. What innate gifts and skills do they bring to the table? How can I help them build upon those natural gifts and skills so that they can become well-rounded contributors to the success of the practice? That's one of the leader's main jobs, in my opinion. It's not about showing them how great I am. It's about showing them how great *they* are and giving them the tools, structure, and opportunities to become even greater.

The longer Jeff, Bryan, and I worked as a team, the more I began to understand how our present and future hierarchy would impact my goal of building a sustainable practice that would thrive with or without me. You know the old saying "climbing the corporate ladder" or "climbing the ladder of success"? I started thinking of the ideal practice structure as a ladder with each of us—Jeff, Bryan, and myself—occupying different rungs.[8]

Image 5.1: Advisor Career Path Ladder

Bryan had started out on the first rung as a client service associate, and initially, Jeff had occupied the third rung, the advisor role, while I taught him the finer points of The Bucket Plan. Initially I had Jeff take over my B-list clients while I retained all my A-list as practicing partner (at that time I was the only practicing partner). Within a year, Jeff had advanced to rung four, lead advisor. Meanwhile, Bryan moved to the second rung, paraplanner, and was advancing quicker than expected under Jeff's guidance. I realized that Jeff was actually perfect to take over my A-list because he's such a fantastic farmer. On the other hand, I am hardwired to hunt. I just want to go out and find more relationships. Together we were the perfect team.

Put another way, the three of us were like trumpet players in an orchestra. I was first chair, and Jeff was my second chair with the A-list. For the B-list, Jeff was the first chair and Bryan second.

---

8   For more information on the career ladder, see the Advisor Career Path chapter beginning on page 107.

For the C-list, Bryan handled that song all by himself. As Jeff and Bryan gained experience performing our practice's unique style of music, they would eventually become good enough horn players to move up a chair with Jeff taking over more of my responsibilities and Bryan taking over more of Jeff's. Then we could add more associate advisors at lower rungs/lower chairs whom we could mentor along the same path.

However, I realized that there's more to this than just visualizing ladders and chairs. For a holistic wealth management practice to become truly sustainable, *all advisors needed to understand precisely what to do to get to the next level* and ultimately (if they are the right fit) achieve partner status. If I could systematize that progression somehow, it would give me—and through C2P, other practice owners—a clear plan for how to grow a self-sustaining company. It would give all the associate advisors a road map to follow, and it would give our clients the peace of mind of knowing that our practice would live on to look after them and their loved ones for generations.

That was the plan. Getting there? That was another thing entirely.

WE NEED HELP!

One afternoon as Jeff and I sat down for a beer, he said he needed to talk to me about a concern he had with Bryan. *Uh oh*, I thought.

"Okay, tell me," I said, preparing myself for bad news. "What's going on with Bryan?"

"He just doesn't have time to help me like he used to," Jeff replied. "I really count on him for support, but we've got him taking over the C-list and doing all these tax returns and Medicare supplements now. He's also starting to win a few financial clients on his own. He's too busy, and I need more help."

"Yeah, that's a problem for sure," I replied.

"And not only that," Jeff continued, "by bringing in new clients, he's creating more work in the backstage. Our support folks are starting to have a tough time keeping up."

"Huh. I guess this is a prime example of being careful what you wish for, eh?"

Jeff shrugged and raised his glass. "Here's to Bryan, for being way too good at his job."

"I'll drink to that!" I said.

In the days that followed, we discussed getting another client service associate (who would ultimately become an advisor) to work the phones, follow up with all the new leads, and do some of the paperwork that Bryan and Jeff didn't have time for. We decided to invest in doing that, but you know me—I wanted to do this thing systematically and in a documented, process-driven way so that it would be efficient and replicable. Luckily, I had the perfect candidate to help me: a friend of mine, Gina Pellegrini, a coach at Strategic Coach and owner of her own successful management consulting firm. She and I sat down and mapped out a process for hiring, onboarding, and training support team members to work in the backstage. We implemented it at JL Smith and also started teaching it to other advisors to see how it worked for them. The process was so impactful that Gina and I wrote a book about it, *The Hiring Advantage*.

The more we helped other advisors implement this hiring process, the more I noticed an unfortunate trend: Practice owners tended to view their support staff as an expense rather than an investment. I remember one owner balking at hiring an assistant at $20-something per hour plus taxes and benefits because she didn't want to part with $50,000 per year. I asked her how much revenue she'd earned the previous year. Her answer: around $500,000.

"Okay, let's assume you worked two thousand hours last year," I said. "That breaks down to you earning about two-hundred-fifty dollars an hour. You're worth two-fifty an hour and you don't want to pay somebody twenty bucks to take over the menial backstage things you're currently doing? That fifty grand will free you to go out and hunt for new opportunities and provide even better service to your clients. It is an *investment* in your business, not an *expense*. Would you invest twenty-five dollars to make two hundred fifty? Of course you would!"

When I put it to her that way, she started to see things differently. She made the investment and reaped the rewards. That's the kind of paradigm shift that needs to happen if you want to grow.

For me, bringing in the right support people and training them in a systematic, process-driven way made a huge difference in our practice. It bought Jeff, Bryan, and me the gift of time—time to do what we do best. It showed how hiring people is not an expense, but an investment—an investment that would ultimately pay off in a very big way.

BRYAN'S ANNUAL REVIEW

By now Bryan had been with us for about five years and he was learning a lot. He was killing it with the Medicare supplements and the tax returns. He had earned his licenses and moved up to the advisor rung, so he had actually started meeting with people and bringing in a steady stream of smaller clients. He was supposed to bring in Jeff to help with anyone with over $500,000 in investable assets, but he didn't always do that. A few times he tried to close them on his own and it didn't work out, which was a little frustrating for Jeff and me. Bryan was like a wild race horse trying to break out of the gate. We had to rein him in occasionally, but all in all, his performance was outstanding considering his brief time in the industry. I was looking forward to his annual review because I knew it was going to be a positive experience for both of us.

On the appointed day, I kicked things off by asking him the famous "Dan Sullivan Question™," which goes like this:

> If we were having this discussion three years from today and you were to look back over those three years to today, what has to have happened, both personally and professionally, for you to feel happy about your progress?

Bryan's response, with no hesitation: "For me to feel happy with my progress in three years, I'd need to be the number one advisor in all of C2P."

Number one advisor? At first I just sat there with this big goofy grin because I thought he was joking. I mean, Bryan was a hard worker and the clients liked him, but in my mind he was still several years away. He only had about $500,000 in AUM and had written a grand total of $700,000 in annuities.

But hey, everybody should have a dream, right? I wasn't about to crush Bryan's confidence, so I kept smiling and said something encouraging like, "Yeah man, you can do it!" But in reality, I was already thinking of ways to help the kid deal with the disappointment of not meeting that insane goal.

THE BIRTH OF A MARKETING PLAN

Our practice was really growing. We were getting loads of referrals from centers of influence and existing clients because of our strong, unique holistic planning process. Our Medicare and tax models were taking off, and we were converting lots of people into financial services clients. I really wanted to help Jeff realize his goal of being number one—he was such a terrific planner—and Bryan was becoming more capable every day. I needed to get them in front of more people. I realized that I had to learn how to do marketing . . . and fast.

It may surprise you, but up to that point in my career I had never done any type of public marketing. I had never hosted a dinner seminar or educational workshop. For me it was all about referrals and cross-selling our tax preparation and Medicare services as a way to open the door to financial planning and wealth management. It had worked well thus far, yet I knew that there was more out there for us if I could only figure out how to spread the word. I didn't want to do our marketing in a haphazard way, though. I'd watched too many other advisors burn through a lot of time and money chasing the next shiny object when it came to marketing their practices, and I was determined not to follow that path.

Having said that, we did try the "free steak dinner seminar" approach . . . once. Bryan and Jeff worked on the content together, and we publicized the event far and wide. We held it at a steak house, and I sat in the audience to take notes to help Bryan and Jeff improve their presentation. Quite a few people showed up, but we soon discovered that most of them were members of one of these three less-than-desirable groups:

- Plate lickers (just there for a free meal),

- Tire kickers (curious but not serious about hiring us), and

- DIYers (looking for tips and tricks so that they could, well, do it themselves).

You've probably guessed by now that our seminar marketing strategy didn't go very well. Not only did we attract the wrong people, but Jeff and Bryan felt awkward the whole time. Forcing themselves to be showmen up on a stage . . . it was unnatural. They were used to educating people, not entertaining and selling to them.

At that point we pivoted toward building a marketing plan and upgrading our online presence. We started doing adult education sessions at colleges and libraries on topics like Social Security, estate planning, taxes, and so on. Adult education was a natural fit for us because our process is instructive. By taking the educational approach versus hosting the typical free steak dinner seminar, we were able to weed out the usual suspects who were only there to take up space. People who enroll in educational programs tend to be more serious than the dinner seminar set. They're not there to fill their bellies on your dime. They're there to fill their minds and learn something valuable.

Sure, we still got a few DIYers at our workshops. But since we were charging the appropriate hourly and flat fees for our planning services, we were making money from those folks too. Many, once they realized how complex this type of planning is, threw in the towel and hired us. It reminds me of the movie *Tommy Boy* when Tommy's dad humorously states the line, "I can get a hell of a good look at a T-bone steak by sticking my head up a bull's ass, but I'd rather take the butcher's word for it."

Shifting from free steak dinners to teaching workshops at colleges and libraries gave us instant credibility and helped us overcome the perception that we were only there to sell something. Since our content was focused solely on delivering useful information in an academic setting, people came to our workshops, learned a lot, and had a great experience. Our reputation in the community got even stronger. People saw us as ethical educators providing valuable content on a wide variety of important financial topics. It was just the cut of beef the butcher ordered.

JEFF'S DISBELIEF

One day around 2014, C2P announced the awards for the top-producing office nationwide, with the top-producing advisor in that office getting the honor of accepting the award. We usually competed for first place with Don Chamberlin's office, and that year I'd told Pablo and Dave not to tell me who won so I could be surprised. And what a surprise it was. Imagine my delight when the top office award was announced and the winner was JL Smith, and not only that: *Jeff Warnkin was named the leading producer in our office and therefore the number one advisor for our financial institution!*

I still chuckle when I recall the day we got that news. You'd think that the guy who'd dreamed of being number one would be shouting and running around the office high-fiving everybody when he found out he'd made it, but no. Jeff just sat there expressionless. I believe he was in shock. I clapped him on the back and said, "Man, I told you that you'd be number one someday, remember?" And he looked at me in total disbelief.

For the next few years as we battled it out with Chamberlin, JL Smith would flip-flop with being named the nation's top-producing office, and Jeff would be named top advisor more than once. If you were to ask him the key to his success, he would tell you without hesitation: The Bucket Plan Process.

BRYAN'S PROMISE

The night before my open-heart surgery, Holly and I and some of our closest friends and business partners went out to dinner in downtown Cleveland. That evening is kind of a blur because of all the thoughts swirling around in my head, but there was one moment that I will never forget. Bryan pulled me off to the side away from the group. He looked me in the eye and told me how grateful he was for everything I'd done for him, for giving him a chance and mentoring him and teaching him how to hunt. And then he told me not to worry, that no matter what happened in that operating room he would make sure that my wife and kids were safe and taken care of financially, and he and Jeff would see to it that JL Smith carried on according to my vision.

"You took care of me, and now it's time for me to take care of you," he said.

To this day, recalling that conversation brings a flood of emotions.

A VISION BECOMES REALITY

Unfortunately for me and my family, things didn't go as planned in the operating room the next day. As I explained in the introduction, my surgery was not successful, and what should have been a two-week recovery period stretched into five long months at home, totally separated from my thriving holistic wealth management practice and C2P. To keep things as stress-free as possible for me while I recovered, my doctors would order me to have no contact with my business team for the entire time I was out. No calls, no emails, no meetings, no texts . . . nothing. For those five months I focused on my recovery and my newly expanded family after the birth of our twins.

Image 5.2: Bryan took this picture of me in downtown Cleveland the night before my surgery. He had it framed and gave it to me as a gift.

Truth be told, when I returned to the office and learned that my practice had its second most profitable quarter ever while I was gone, I had mixed feelings. To find out that the world had continued to spin without me being there to hold it up on my shoulders like some almighty Atlas . . . well, that was kind of humbling, to be honest. But once the shock wore off and I was able to set my ego aside, the magnitude of what we had accomplished became clear. We truly had built a self-sustaining holistic wealth management practice that flourished without me—the founder and original rainmaker—being there. JL Smith would not only survive but thrive in a spectacular way for decades to come. My clients' best interests would be served for generations, and my family's security was assured. My vision had become reality.

THE MAKING OF A SUPERSTAR

Oh, and there was one more surprising newsflash that the team relayed to me on my first day back in the office: While I was out, *Bryan had become the top producer on the leaderboard!* He truly did step up and take care of business just like he said he would. I won't even try to describe how great that felt as a mentor. There are simply no words.

You see this in professional sports a lot, where all of a sudden the superstar goes down and a bench player rises to the occasion and becomes a superstar in their own right. Forever a superstar . . . that's Bryan. For five years in a row now he has been the number one producer in the country for C2P. Bryan is the hardest working man in show business. He's the James Brown of financial planning. He'll outwork any person in existence, putting in all the grit, blood, sweat, and tears required to get the job done. If you can find yourself a Bryan—a rookie bench player with great potential—grab 'em and invest in developing them. They hold the golden key to the future of your practice.

As for Jeff, we nicknamed him "The Wizard" because he is a tax magician. This guy checks all the boxes and then some. It's incredibly humbling just thinking about the body of knowledge he's worked so hard to accumulate. Jeff's very methodical and organized, and he follows processes to a T. His view is that if something works, don't mess with it. With the temperament of a kind uncle, he was the perfect day-to-day mentor for our wild child Bryan. Bryan will be the first to tell you that when it comes to taxes, Jeff taught him everything he knows. If you can find yourself a Jeff—a highly skilled technician to serve as the steady backbone of your practice—grab 'em. They have the know-how to help you mentor and develop your team's future stars.

A PERFECT PICTURE

Picture a day when your firm is this profitable without your production. Or when you have an advisor that you've trained, developed, and mentored say, "Thank you for changing my life." Or maybe it's when you get to take a month-long dream vacation with no phone calls or emails.

Whether you're just starting out on this journey, in the middle, or you're feeling stuck, we want to help you—I want to help you!

You never know what life is going to throw at you. In addition to what I've shared in this story, in 2015, my wife Holly and I had our first set of twins, Berkeley and Wyatt, when I was on my doctor-ordered five-month leave. I got to spend three of those months with the new twins and support my wife like she has supported me. Then in 2017, our second set of twins, Lincoln and Lennon, were born, and I took five months off—no interaction with the team, no communication with clients other than friendly interactions, no business whatsoever.

By developing and implementing a series of first-rate processes and creating and cultivating an environment for the right people—one a seasoned veteran and the other a diamond in the rough—I truly was able to multiply my capacity as a rainmaker and build my business to run successfully with or without me.

You can do the same. You deserve **financial freedom** for your business to take care of your spouse, your family, and yourself. You deserve **relationship freedom** to not have to take care of the clients that do not give you energy any longer. You deserve **time freedom** to be able to have your business work for you, not the opposite. You deserve **freedom**.

The remainder of this book will give you the elements of this winning formula.

PART II

The Rainmaker Multiplier Essentials

What if you could do what I did with Jeff and Bryan and replicate your capabilities so that your business would run profitably with or without you? As my story illustrates, it can be done. In fact, it *is* being done right now all across the country by advisors like you who are following the Rainmaker Multiplier Proven Process and Platform.

There's a journey that most advisors go through as they build their careers, and this journey is reflected in our model's four quadrants:

Image II.1: The Rainmaker Multiplier Proven Process and Platform

The very first thing we learn is to implement a sales process to get the people we meet to do business with us. For me, that sales process has been **holistic planning** using The Bucket Plan.

Once we've mastered our sales process, a light bulb tends to go off, and we realize that one-on-one prospecting and sales are not enough. Sure, we can grow on referrals, but we don't have much direct control over that. It's well-executed marketing that gives us our desired degree of scalability. We need to figure out how to market to groups and find the people who *want* to meet with us so that we can eliminate the constant rejection and wasted time that can come from one-on-one prospecting. We need a **marketing plan and strategy** that creates a steady flow of new opportunities.

The longer we spend in the industry, we find more diverse ways to not only make more revenue, but also to better serve our clients. As we gain traction in our careers, most of us look for new **profitable business lines** like charging financial planning fees, adding (or enhancing) a tax practice, or adding Medicare supplement services, for example, so that we can expand our reach even further.

Then, if we get really good at doing holistic planning, implementing smart and cost-effective marketing plans, and opening more profitable business lines, forget about it . . . we're off to the races! We no longer have the capacity to attend to all of our existing clients, let alone add new ones. Now we have a choice to make: We either slow down the marketing or we grow our practice by bringing in additional advisors and increasing our support staff. In other words, we learn how to run a business—or what we call **practice management**. This, arguably, is the hardest thing to figure out on your own.

So, holistic planning, marketing planning and strategy, profitable business lines, and practice management—those are the four quadrants of the Rainmaker Multiplier Proven Process and Platform. The RMM—which sprang from my own experience and that of other top producers—is for advisors with high growth aspirations who want to create a self-sustaining company and increase their net profitability. It turns great financial advisors like you into even greater business owners. The RMM was built by advisors, for advisors. It helps you define your vision and then take the necessary steps to accomplish your goals without sacrificing your work/life balance. Helping you build a company that can run successfully on its own—that's the purpose of the RMM.

Here in Part II, we begin at the heart of the RMM Proven Process and Platform by exploring the various elements of **Holistic Financial Planning**. Then we move on to the remaining three RMM Essentials: **Marketing Planning and Strategy**, the **Tax Model**, and the **Advisor Career Path**. As you can see in the illustration above, there's more to the model than just these four essentials. Don't worry, we'll get to the rest of it in Part III!

When you implement these processes and use these platforms, your practice will thrive and become scalable. Your family's future will be secured and your clients will be well-served by your firm for generations.

First up: the elements necessary to create true holistic financial plans.

CHAPTER 6

Holistic Financial Planning

A lot has changed since my father started his career back in the 1970s. Come to think of it, a lot has changed in this industry in just the past decade or so. Thanks to the internet, information is more abundant and accessible than ever before, making it seem as if any layperson can do their own research and financial planning. More banks and custodians have gotten into financial services, causing a commoditization of our profession and a substantial drop in fees and commissions. Financial institutions are popping up on every street corner because everyone can see what's happening: A tsunami of asset transfers is crashing in, and opportunists want to take advantage. The monster wealth transfer that's taking place (and that is going to continue over the next several years) has caught everyone's attention. The result? A market that is oversaturated and tremendously competitive.

It has become increasingly difficult for independent advisors like you and me to remain relevant in this crazy environment because there's just way too much cheap competition out there selling the same old products in the same old way. Traditional financial products salespeople are a dime a dozen. And since our ideal clients are becoming more financially savvy every day, they naturally expect their advisors to do more for them than they can do on their own. The only way we're going to stay alive and grow is to differentiate ourselves and our value propositions so we can attract and keep high-net-worth clients. In my experience, the surest way to do that is to switch to a planning fee–based business model and adopt a professional, process-driven, holistic approach to service delivery. That approach has five components: (1) The Bucket Plan, (2) tax planning and management, (3) estate planning, (4) investment management, and (5) insurance and annuities.

THE BUCKET PLAN

TAX PLANNING AND MANAGEMENT— ESTATE PLANNING—INVESTMENT MANAGEMENT— INSURANCE AND ANNUITIES

Before Jeff joined JL Smith, he was a nervous wreck going into meetings with prospective clients. What would he say to them? How could he explain his value proposition? Was he going to fumble his words this time? He didn't have a system or a repeatable process, and it showed. But once he started following our proven Bucket Plan planning process, his confidence soared and his stress level went way down. These days, he has two or three opening appointments every day and he knows exactly what he's going to do each time because he has a repeatable process. Doesn't matter if the prospect is coming to him through the tax practice or if they're a Medicare lead or if they came in through our Social Security workshop. Doesn't matter what the source is. Jeff goes through the exact same presentation the same way every time, because The Bucket Plan document guides him (see images 6.1 and 6.2).

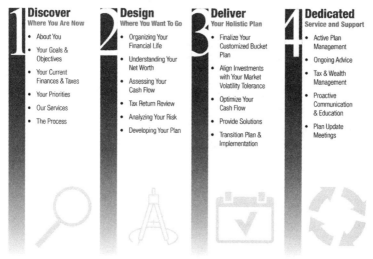

The Bucket Plan®
Holistic Planning in Your Best Interest

1 Discover
Where You Are Now
- About You
- Your Goals & Objectives
- Your Current Finances & Taxes
- Your Priorities
- Our Services
- The Process

2 Design
Where You Want To Go
- Organizing Your Financial Life
- Understanding Your Net Worth
- Assessing Your Cash Flow
- Tax Return Review
- Analyzing Your Risk
- Developing Your Plan

3 Deliver
Your Holistic Plan
- Finalize Your Customized Bucket Plan
- Align Investments with Your Market Volatility Tolerance
- Optimize Your Cash Flow
- Provide Solutions
- Transition Plan & Implementation

4 Dedicated
Service and Support
- Active Plan Management
- Ongoing Advice
- Tax & Wealth Management
- Proactive Communication & Education
- Plan Update Meetings

Image 6.1: The Bucket Plan List

Prepared for: _____ Date: _____	Deliverables
Retirement Income Distribution Plan	
Goals Based Financial Plan	
Volatility Tolerance & Investment Alignment	
Periodic Review Meeting	
Proactive Wealth Management	
Cash Flow Assessment	
Social Security Optimization	
Pension Maximization	
401(k) and Qualified Plan Allocation Analysis	
Investment Audit	
General Financial Advice	
Financial Modeling Report	
Medical / Medicare[1] Insurance Evaluation	
Long Term Care / Disability Risk Mitigation	
Life Insurance Audit / Needs Analysis	
Charitable Giving Strategies	
The Family Estate Organizer	
Beneficiary Designation Review & Update	
The Family Succession Plan	
Estate Planning Document Review[2]	
Estate Tax Reduction	
Probate Avoidance Strategies	
Annual Tax Loss / Gain Harvesting	
Roth Conversion Bracket Bumping	
Prior Year Tax Return Review	
Income Tax Reduction Strategies	
Your Customized Bucket Plan	

[1] For Clients 65 and older
[2] Legal document review provided by independent counsel; update to documents may require additional fee.

Cost: $

REV. 12-06-2021

Image 6.2: Deliverables

We laminate this two-sided document and keep it on the table to use as a prop during our meetings. It's presented as a four-step process, but the bulk of the initial planning is really done in the first three, as step four is onboarding and service. On the surface it doesn't look that different from what we are all taught when we come into the business: establish rapport, gather data, establish goals and objectives, present solutions, and close. But here, the real game changer is that second step, where we build the Family Estate Organizer. This is what transforms you in the prospect's eyes. Now, instead of selling products, you're making it all about them. You're organizing and educating them about what they have and are doing a deep dive into where they want to go.

However, let's back up to that all-important first step: making the connection and discovering where they are now. We all know that the hardest part of any new client relationship is getting them to agree to move forward. So, visit **RMMbook.com/toolkit** and spend some time exploring our guide to the first step of The Bucket Plan process, the initial appointment, because that's where the magic happens. Here you'll learn tips for establishing rapport, how to know when it's time to launch the sales process, which specific questions to ask, how to quote your planning fee, and how to close. You'll also get access to our checklists and the components of the Family Estate Organizer.

Now we turn our attention to the next essential piece for creating holistic plans: tax planning and management.

THE BUCKET PLAN
. . . .

TAX PLANNING AND MANAGEMENT— ESTATE PLANNING—INVESTMENT MANAGEMENT— INSURANCE AND ANNUITIES

It's not what you make, it's what you keep. That's our mantra as holistic wealth managers. That's why tax implications and mitigation strategies are critical considerations for all of our investment advice. Most people only think of taxes when it is time to write a check to the IRS, but ideally, tax planning and management is a year-round process. From putting a plan in place to fund estimated tax liabilities, to monitoring investment transactions so they don't cause the wrong type of tax, to managing proper investment types to maximize after-tax returns, proper tax planning and management adds substantial wealth to your clients and their families over time.

But the current United States tax code and revenue rulings are over 74,000 pages long. Complexity is greater today than it has ever been, and the IRS isn't very forgiving if we make mistakes. Within those 74,000 pages, there are hundreds of ways to reduce or eliminate our clients' current and future tax burden, but how to even begin to untangle it all?

Simplifying the complex . . . that's our job. At the end of the day there are only two types of taxes: unavoidable taxes and avoidable taxes. Unavoidable taxes are legally what we have to pay. It's in black and white in the IRS tax code. Avoidable taxes, on the other hand, are taxes that can be averted through proper planning or strategy. We want to help our clients eliminate the avoidable taxes. That was the driving force for creating the Tax Management Journey. The Tax Management Journey is a systematic process engineered to not only reduce your clients' taxation today, but also into the future. To be a holistic advisor, you surely need to incorporate tax planning and management into your approach. The Tax Management Journey was built to give advisors a simple, proven process to take their clients through—a process that takes some people a lifetime to figure out.

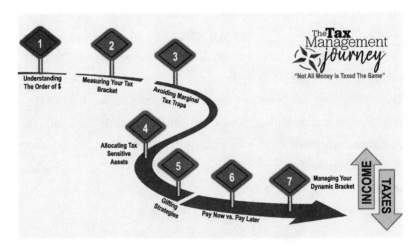

Image 6.3: The Tax Management Journey

Our online guide to the Tax Management Journey at RMMbook .com/toolkit will give you the tools to educate your clients about "the order of money." It will show you how to measure a client's tax bracket, avoid marginal tax traps, and allocate tax-sensitive assets. It will help you understand gifting strategies and the big-picture question of "pay now or pay later." And finally, you'll learn how to teach your clients the difference between tax planning, tax management, and tax preparation so you can really drive home the value of having you there to help them manage their dynamic tax bracket as life, political, and economic changes evolve.

The Tax Management Journey will help you attract and retain more affluent clients. It's a defensive move for your business because if you're not providing this service to your clients, they're going to go to somebody else to get it. Much of the business we get at JL Smith is because people are looking for tax management help, but we don't provide that unless they are a wealth management client, as it is critical to have access to their assets to effectively manage their tax situation year-round. Once they see that they can have one trusted advisor coordinating everything for them under one roof, they'll be all in, and they'll start telling other people about your one-stop shop.

As the good word about your practice begins to spread throughout the community, your networking success will increase exponentially. Other professionals—attorneys, CPAs, and the like—will want to partner with you, and one of the most important partnerships you can form is with an attorney.

Which brings us to . . .

THE BUCKET PLAN
. . . .

TAX PLANNING AND MANAGEMENT—
ESTATE PLANNING—INVESTMENT MANAGEMENT—
INSURANCE AND ANNUITIES

As financial advisors, most of us have investment and insurance licenses. Some of us have a tax background, but not many of us have a law degree and are able to draw up estate planning documents. That means we have to partner with an attorney at some point in the estate planning process. If you're going to partner with an attorney, you might as well leverage that relationship and make the most of it. Sounds easy, but that's not always the case.

Years ago I had an attorney to whom I was referring an incredible amount of business. He was doing a great job for my clients, but he wasn't referring anyone to me. Then I developed the Attorney Advisor Alliance™ process with the National Network of Estate Planning Attorneys and tried the system with a different attorney. He's now a $3 million AAA client who consistently refers new business to us.

Do you have an attorney right now who is a client, a raving fan, and is consistently referring people to you? If you do, congratulations. You already know why an alliance with an attorney is such a great advantage. If you don't, *you need to go through this process ASAP.*

Our industry is shifting, and today's consumer is looking for their professionals to communicate, collaborate, and coordinate all aspects of their financial and estate plans. We know we need to bring other professionals into the planning mix from time to time, which is why we establish referral partners. But there is a significant difference between a referral partner and a professional alliance. With a referral partner, the collaboration generally stops once the referral is given. It is purely transactional. Most advisors fail to capitalize on the value of the professional relationship development process before and after that mutual client is served. By shifting the relationship from a referral partner into a professional alliance, you can transform your business by providing better advice and service, gaining a true collaborative partner to help you grow, reducing marketing expenses, and getting in front of more ideal clients.

This is why we created the Attorney Advisor Alliance—Referral Matchmaking System. Whether you have an existing attorney/advisor relationship or you are seeking a new one, the Attorney Advisor Alliance four-step process will help you achieve greater success.

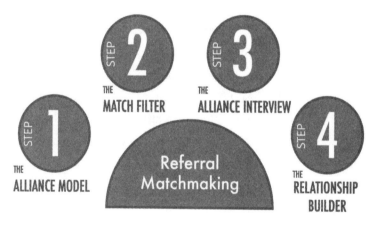

Image 6.4: Referral Matchmaking

Our guide to the Attorney Advisor Alliance discusses how to tap into your existing client base and centers of influence to get recommendations for a professional with whom to create an alliance. We outline the steps for researching those professionals, doing in-person meetings, conducting interviews, narrowing your decision down to a select few attorneys or advisors, and building and maintaining a strong relationship with the one(s) you choose so that you share referrals and do joint client-appreciation events and marketing that benefit you both. Creating this kind of alliance will not only grow your business but provide a more well-rounded service to your clients.

Get our guide to the Attorney Advisor Alliance right here: RMMbook.com/toolkit

THE BUCKET PLAN

. . . .

TAX PLANNING AND MANAGEMENT— ESTATE PLANNING—*INVESTMENT MANAGEMENT*— INSURANCE AND ANNUITIES

When I think of the philosophy of creating holistic financial plans, it reminds me of building a new house. I can find the best architect in town to draw up the blueprint for me, but even though this blueprint was created by an expert, I can't implement it. I suppose I could try. I could go to Home Depot and buy a hammer and a box of nails and some lumber, but what good would that do? I know nothing about building a house. I don't have the technical capability. I need a contractor, a foreman, an electrician, a plumber, and so on. Without them, that beautiful blueprint isn't worth anything to me at all.

It's not enough for us to deliver stellar holistic plans to our clients. We also need to be able to facilitate and implement those plans, and that's where investment vehicles come into play. This is a big deal because the investment piece of a client's portfolio is generally their largest piece. Years ago, people didn't have to worry about investments so much because they worked for a company their whole career and had a big pension when they retired. Since the invention of the 401k, pensions have pretty much gone away. Investments are the main pillar of how people retire today. The problem is that there are so many choices and investment options out there that advisors sometimes get overwhelmed trying to figure out how to pick the best solution for their clients' goals and objectives.

That's why we built a single platform for advisors to be able to implement their investment recommendations for their clients . . . a curated list of options to help you simplify that complex decision. In essence, we provide an agnostic institutional investment platform so you can deliver turnkey model portfolio solutions (in addition to customized portfolio strategies) to help your clients achieve the goals and objectives of their holistic financial plan.

If you're doing holistic planning, you are, as a necessity, going to have to be investment licensed and advising your clients on their investment holdings, portfolios, and allocations. By nature of that necessity, you then have to decide if you're going to be an investment manager or if you're going to outsource and delegate the investment management so you can focus on client relationships and holistic planning. We've built a platform that can help accommodate advisors in either position. Whether you want to leverage some of the largest and most renowned institutional professional money managers as a turnkey solution, or you want to deliver customized solutions and investment management to your clients yourself, we've simplified the process so that whichever camp you're in, we make it easier to do business and implement Bucket Plans.

You can read all about it in our guide to investments here: RMMbook.com/toolkit

THE BUCKET PLAN

. . . .

TAX PLANNING AND MANAGEMENT—
ESTATE PLANNING—INVESTMENT MANAGEMENT—
INSURANCE AND ANNUITIES

In a nutshell, insurance and annuities are products that we use as financial planning tools. Advisors and insurance professionals who are not planners are going to lead with selling these types of products. On the other side of the aisle are those of us who utilize The Bucket Plan. We lead with the plan, and the plan sells the products for us. That's because as we're building the plan, the client's risks are exposed. We educate the client on those risks and then offer solutions to mitigate them, to insure them. The way we insure income-related risk while the client is living is through annuities. The way we insure income-related risk when they're deceased is through life insurance. It's really that simple.

Let's talk about insurance first.

INSURANCE

We don't do a lot of term life insurance unless it's all the client can afford and/or it's being utilized specifically to cover debt and income replacement for someone with a long runway before retirement. We most often recommend permanent life insurance to those in or near retirement for two very good reasons. First, we want our clients to own it versus renting it. We want to make sure that the money is going to be there when the time comes, so their survivors will get what was intended for them. There's no expiration date on permanent like there is on term. The second reason we prefer permanent is that it accumulates cash value that can be leveraged to access growth on our client's money, tax-free.

But which type of permanent insurance to recommend . . . whole life or indexed universal life? We don't use variable products. The primary difference between whole life insurance and indexed universal life insurance is the structure of the insurance policy itself. Whole life insurance has been around for over a generation and is a time-tested way to insure against premature death while building cash value as a savings vehicle. The insurance companies structure the policies so that you pay a certain amount of premium for a certain period of time, and the policy is meant to endow (cash value equals death benefit) upon a certain age (typically age 100). The underlying guarantees of a whole life insurance policy are among the highest guarantees in life insurance, and because those underlying guarantees are higher, the amount of premium needed for one dollar of death benefit tends to be higher than its associated counterpart, indexed universal life.

A whole life insurance company may pay a dividend to its policy owners. That dividend could be viewed as a return of premium for the results or the performance that the insurance company has attained for that given year. For example, if the insurance company has strong performance, meaning they collected more premiums than they paid out in death benefit and their insurance portfolio earned a rate of return that they were happy about, they would pay a dividend to the policyholders to reward them for continuing to hold their life insurance policy. That dividend is not guaranteed, but some of the biggest and strongest whole life insurance companies have paid a dividend continuously for many decades.

In contrast, an indexed universal life insurance policy has lower guarantees than the counterpart whole life insurance policy. Because the guarantees are less, the initial required premium is, in many cases, lower and, in order to ensure the indexed universal life policy doesn't lapse, it generally needs to meet a certain performance rate of return on the cash value in the policy.

The performance of an indexed universal life policy is generated by electing a fixed interest rate option or foregoing the fixed rate and allocating the cash value to indexed interest accounts.

These indexed interest accounts track the underlying stock market indices, such as the S&P 500 index. The client has the ability to participate in the gains of that index up to a certain cap or participation rate, but also has the peace of mind of knowing that there is a floor of zero. In the event the stock market index goes down, they will not lose money due to stock market decreases.

An indexed universal life policy could be viewed as a little bit riskier for the client than its counterpart whole life insurance, but it also could provide the client a higher rate of return to compensate them for that risk. Or, it could mean that the client can pay less premium into the indexed universal life policy to provide for that same one dollar of death benefit.

A big differentiator for the two is that, for clients who want absolute predictability with their life insurance and are willing to pay a potentially higher cost for that predictability, whole life insurance is a great option. For clients who have a little bit more of an appetite for risk or uncertainty, in hopes of greater upside reward based on market index returns, an IUL policy may be more appropriate.

Both policies accumulate cash value inside of them, which could be used for tax-free supplemental income if structured the right way, and many even offer a long-term care rider to accelerate the death benefit in the event that the client needs long-term care.

It's not uncommon for us to present both options to a client, and often they choose both and split the committed premium between two policies.

ANNUITIES

After I've determined how much money a potential client is going to need to draw for income or withdrawals from their Soon bucket, I always ask them how much of their income they want guaranteed. Let's imagine they have to draw $40,000 a year from their Soon bucket to supplement Social Security. I'll ask them how much of that $40,000 worth of income they want guaranteed. Their response in almost every case: "What do you mean by guaranteed?" I then explain that there are only three ways to guarantee income. The first way is through a bank and the FDIC. For example, you can build a CD ladder. The second way is through the federal government with a bond ladder. The third way is through an insurance company, like pensions do. This is an annuity. I then ask them if they have a preference for any one of those, or if they just want the one that will give them the highest potential rate of return while still offering a guarantee. Some people have an aversion to annuities, CDs, or government bonds, and so on, but through this dialogue we'll get an idea of their thinking. This conversation is one of the ways we can find out if a fixed-index annuity may be an appropriate option to provide for the desired income.

At JL Smith we prefer indexed annuities in the Soon bucket for age-appropriate people because they give us the underlying guarantee that the client won't be subjected to sequence of returns risk, or be forced to draw money out when the market is down. They can never make that money back. With an indexed annuity, we index the interest rate off of how well the market performs. If the market and index crediting method does well, we earn a favorable interest rate. If the market does poorly, we simply earn a zero that year, but we don't lose money. We don't subject ourselves to that risk, and there's not a fee drag. We have stability and a reliable income.

Follow this link to learn the difference between whole life versus indexed universal life, the three keys to funding a Soon bucket with annuities, and how to use the "best interest screening process": RMMbook.com/toolkit

. . . .

That wraps up the five elements of holistic planning. Now we move on to the remaining three Rainmaker Multiplier Essentials: marketing planning and strategy, the tax model, and the advisor career path.

CHAPTER 7

Marketing Planning and Strategy

Today at JL Smith, we're knocking the cover off the ball in comparison to most firms. We brought in over $130 million of new assets last year (2023), and over 60% of that came from our marketing funnels. I love this because I'm a control freak; with marketing you have direct control over the results once you know your numbers and have a process down. In other words, you'll get to the point where you know that if you spend X, then Y is going to happen.

That's how it is at our firm. We know exactly how many seminar registrants we need on average to get a certain number of attendees. Out of those attendees, we know how many will book right fit calls. Of those right fit calls, we know how many are going to qualify to work with us. Of those who qualify, we know how many will agree to and actually show up for their first discovery appointment. Out of those who show up, we know the percentage that will agree to pay a planning fee to go through The Bucket Plan process. Of those who go through our process, we know how many will become wealth management and insurance clients.

Yes, we know our numbers very well. Nowadays, when we go through the inevitable ebbs and flows where our current efforts are not producing the number of registrants we need for our desired end result to happen, we can simply dial up our ad spend (we're even able to anticipate when those ebbs and flows will happen). At the same time, we will do some research and development (R&D) and try a different marketing message to see if that can increase our numbers. It's good to have this type of diversification. You don't want to be a one-trick pony relying solely on a single marketing solution, because if something were to interrupt that main thing you're doing, you'd be sunk. A change in a regulation, a new law, or—as we all know—a pandemic can be devastating if you're only doing one type of marketing.

For instance, many advisors were completely reliant on live presentations and face-to-face financial planning before COVID hit. They had a pretty steep learning curve when they suddenly lost the ability to do live business. Those who didn't take action quickly enough suffered, but those who were diversified in the various ways of attracting new business did better. At JL Smith we didn't just shift to webinars. We also built a new marketing strategy/process around them, which has helped us adapt and bring on some of the biggest clients we've ever had. That's why it's good to stay diversified and always be doing research and development into the different ways of getting in front of new people. But, at the end of the day, we're going to keep doing what works. Having a marketing plan and strategy is what got us to this point.

Contrast that with relying on referrals, centers of influence, and cross-selling opportunities off your existing book. No doubt about it, you'll get a certain amount of business from those and you can do well, but you have to control the behavior of your advisors in order to make it work. With a marketing plan and strategy, if you want to fill more calendar space, you simply dial up your investment and watch the results produce themselves.

One caveat, though: You can't just go tossing around marketing money willy-nilly. Yes, a certain part of your budget should be R&D, but the bulk of it should be going toward what works. I see lots of advisors get distracted by shiny objects in the marketing realm—it's very easy to do!—which only leads to frustration and waste. No, you have to formulate and follow a marketing plan and strategy that you can stick to—a plan and strategy that can be scaled for growth. Whether you're one advisor trying to hit your first $1 million in revenue or an established ensemble practice trying to hit $10 million in revenue, you can do this. You *need* to do this!

Our guide to marketing planning and strategy was created with input from some of the top marketing experts in our industry. It gives you the steps to create a solid plan and a concise strategy that works for your budget and your target audience. It helps you define your challenges, set realistic goals, create accountability, and evaluate your results in a meaningful way. In short, it helps you use your resources wisely.

Find the guide at RMMbook.com/toolkit

CHAPTER 8

The Tax Trilogy

Everyone likes a good movie trilogy, right? How about a tax trilogy? Adding tax planning, management, and preparation services is a game changer for your firm, one that's been transformative for me and countless other advisors. It's one phenomenal way to show the people in your community that you are different from the rest of your competition. Most advisors in your area are not doing tax work in their offices, at least not all three facets. Many of them are not even talking about taxes with their clients because their broker dealers won't allow them to. There's a disclaimer on the bottom of every statement they send out saying, "We do not give tax or legal advice." So, having a tax services offering sets you apart from the pack.

You'll recall from earlier when I mentioned that taxes are our single biggest differentiator. It's where we get our best, ideal clients in our firm. That's why we tripled down on it. The key part is getting the messaging down for your ideal client, and it's messaging that a lot of people have a hard time understanding. In particular, it's the difference between tax planning and tax management. Everybody knows what tax preparation is, right? It's basically filling in what happened in the past and having the IRS tell you what the outcome is. But when it comes to tax planning and management, the difference between the two can be confusing. Again, we can use the analogy of building a house. Tax planning is creating the blueprint for the house. Tax management is building and maintaining the house. Tax preparation is then your final inspection. In our firm, clients or prospects can pay us a fee for tax preparation and for tax planning. But we will *not* do the tax management without them becoming a wealth management client of the firm. We will not build the house or maintain the house until they become a wealth management client of the firm.

So you can see how these have become the cornerstone of our lead generation efforts. The tax management has become the best hook, but it's not possible without the tax planning and preparation pieces. We call it the **Tax Trilogy**.

One of the most valuable aspects of tax preparation is the referrals you get from doing tax returns. People will refer much more readily to a tax service than they will to a financial advisor. We get hundreds of referrals a year to our tax service, and we're meeting more new people in our community every season. In fact, we've become selective about which tax clients we'll take on. Consequently, our wealth management business has expanded exponentially.

But . . . where to start? We've created a model centered on three different ways you can incorporate this essential element of a tax practice into your organization. You can either build it, buy it, or borrow it. It's up to you. No single option is better or worse than the others. It all comes down to which one best fits your unique situation, your practice, and your personality.

Before we dig into the options, let me make one point crystal clear:

> You shouldn't add a tax prep business line unless you intend to do tax planning along with it (which will ultimately lead to financial planning). Doing tax prep without tax planning is like promoting a loss leader that doesn't actually lead to anything.

Now let's explore your tax practice options.

You can do what we did at JL Smith, which was to **BUILD** a practice. The hardest part was getting started, so with the help of our tax practice building experts at C2P, we created an eight-step process and all the tools to help you become a true tax advisor to your clients and even do taxes in your office. The process guides you through laying the groundwork for your new tax practice by helping you set up your office, systems, documents, technology, and training. It covers finding and selecting the right professional(s) to do your tax preparation, marketing your new service, setting appointments, meeting tax prep clients, and converting them into wealth management clients. It's truly a fantastic A–Z guide for building a tax practice.

Rather than going through the building process, some advisors prefer to **BUY** an established tax practice and just fold it into their financial services firm. We've seen a healthy surge of advisors wanting to buy tax practices lately, so we did it ourselves and then created a system for how to do it. It covers finding and evaluating accounting firms that are for sale, how to approach them and set yourself apart from the scores of other potential buyers, how to conduct due diligence, and even how to structure the financing.

I recognize that not everyone is ready, willing, or able to build or buy a tax practice. If that's your situation, you can always **BORROW** one. Borrowing a tax practice is common in our industry. Basically it's a process similar to the Attorney Advisor Alliance—you're just doing it with a CPA firm. Most of you reading this book are already generating business through a CPA or accounting firm relationship. The reason I've included this option is that there's a myth that if you have a tax business like we do, you can't also have a CPA as a center of influence or a referral source, and that's false. We're living proof. Within three years of borrowing our first tax practice, we generated over $20 million of new assets out of their office.

The story of how our "Borrow It" situation came to pass—along with our "Build It" and "Buy It" systems—is told in our free online guide to the tax model. Check it out right here:

RMMbook.com/toolkit

Now we come to the final RMM essential—how to multiply your capacity as a rainmaker by establishing a career path and mentoring for your firm's existing and future advisors.

CHAPTER 9

The Advisor Career Path

My late father dispensed a lot of sage advice to me over the years, advice that's served me really well. One of the best nuggets of wisdom Dad ever gave me was this: *Never do anything that you can pay someone else to do for less money than what you can make in the same amount of time.* He told me this when I was tiny, as early as I can remember. It got me in the mindset of calculating, from a very young age, how much my time was worth. That's why when I was in my early twenties and bought my first house, I paid someone to mow my lawn. Most people that age would never have done that. None of my neighbors—not even those in their fifties and sixties—were paying for lawn maintenance, but I knew that I could use those few hours a month to make more money than it cost me to have someone else cut the grass.

There was a problem with my thinking, though . . . I tried to pay the very least amount of money possible to get things done, even in my business. Early in my career I had a lot of turnover in advisors, assistants, and staff because I was underpaying people. I wasn't able to articulate that they had the ability to earn their way to advancement in their career and compensation. Then I had a shift in mindset and realized that people are an *investment*, not an *expense*. If you can attract, retain, and reward the right people, the sky's the limit for how successful you can be. But you know what? You really shouldn't be thinking about how successful you're going to be. You should be thinking about how successful you can make them. Because when they succeed, so will you. Automatically.

> They say the most critical factor for the success of any business is its ability to attract, retain, and reward talent. That has certainly been the case for me.

By leveraging the talent on your team and adopting a career path structure for your advisors, your business will grow faster, achieve higher levels of profitability, attract larger client relationships, and establish your legacy for your surviving spouse and loved ones. This will enable you to build a succession plan and give your clients the peace of mind of knowing that your practice will live on to look after them and their families for generations.

Our process shows you how to clearly communicate your firm's career path to existing advisors and new recruits. We set out the milestones for progression through the rungs of the career ladder from entry level to practicing partner, and we help you establish accountability at every step. Our process and coaching help you decide whether to recruit for a "hunter" or a "farmer" to enable growth, and it covers how to mentor them along the path.

Identifying whether you need someone who's great at farming

or hunting and then plugging that person into a proven career path where they can be mentored all the way to the top and then mentor others—that's how you scale your business to run profitably, seamlessly, the way you want it to, even when you're not there. Having a well-developed career path will improve your recruiting outcomes and strengthen your team. With the right people in the right seats—each with a clear understanding of their individual road map for success—your firm will become an unstoppable force.

Follow this link to get our guide to the advisor career path:

RMMbook.com/toolkit

PART III

Choose Your Own Adventure: Rainmaker Multiplier Building Blocks

This is the perfect moment to stop and reflect. If you've read the whole book up to this point, you know that building a self-sustaining holistic wealth management practice is not easy. You've read about how my team and I busted our butts to achieve this unbelievable milestone. But if you skipped straight to this page without reading the preceding chapters (hello, rebel!), you don't yet know everything we went through to get here. Trust me, it was hard work. Years and years of hard work and sacrifice.

This kind of undertaking is not for everyone. It's definitely not for the faint of heart.

Whether you are ready to launch the RMM immediately or need a little more time to wrap your head around it, fill out our Challenges and Priorities Worksheet to illuminate your path forward. This worksheet will clarify the issues in your unique business that most need your attention. Think of this as similar to a kitchen stove. The items on the front burner are the most important, the things you've got to address right away. These are the "1s" on the worksheet. The "2s" are on the back burners. They're important, they're on the stove . . . but they're just simmering. They don't need immediate attention. And then there are the "3s." They're not even in the kitchen, let alone on the stove. You don't need to worry about them. So, complete the worksheet, identify your priorities, and then read on to learn about the additional resources we've created to help you tackle them. Remember: You're going to choose your own adventure and create your own ending to this story. The worksheet in image III.1 will point the way.

CHALLENGES & PRIORITIES
RANKING WORKSHEET

Date:_____ **Advisor Name(s)** _____

Please rank each item below from 1 to 3 (1=biggest challenge, and 3=not a challenge)

Ranking	**Challenges & Priorities**	**Notes**

Marketing & Business Development

○ 1 ○ 2 ○ 3 I'm not seeing enough new prospects _____

○ 1 ○ 2 ○ 3 I need a proven process to ask for
and track referrals _____

○ 1 ○ 2 ○ 3 Marketing to the prospects in my existing
database is not as good as it could be _____

○ 1 ○ 2 ○ 3 I need a marketing plan to stay focused
and measure results of my marketing efforts _____

○ 1 ○ 2 ○ 3 I want to improve my online marketing
presence and platform _____

○ 1 ○ 2 ○ 3 I want to get better at creating content _____

○ 1 ○ 2 ○ 3 I need a process to engage and track COIs _____

○ 1 ○ 2 ○ 3 I have clearly defined business
development processes _____

Holistic Planning

○ 1 ○ 2 ○ 3 I'm not converting enough prospects from the
first appointment to go through the process _____

○ 1 ○ 2 ○ 3 I need to simplify my planning process and
deliverable to the client _____

○ 1 ○ 2 ○ 3 I'm spending too much time educating and
building financial plans and not getting
paid for my time _____

○ 1 ○ 2 ○ 3 I want to get better at tax planning
& management _____

○ 1 ○ 2 ○ 3 I don't have a solid system to work my client
base for cross-selling opportunities _____

CHALLENGES & PRIORITIES
RANKING WORKSHEET

Ranking	Challenges & Priorities	Notes
Profitable Business Lines		
○1　○2　○3	I need training and/or sales support to place more life insurance	_____
○1　○2　○3	I need training and/or sales support to place more asset-based long-term care	_____
○1　○2　○3	I need more sales ideas and information on new annuity products and carriers	_____
○1　○2　○3	I need to improve my AUM story/pitch deck	_____
○1　○2　○3	I'm frustrated by my current Broker Dealer/RIA placing restrictions on the way I do business	_____
○1　○2　○3	I'm worried about the increased fiduciary responsibility placed on me by regulators	_____
○1　○2　○3	I would like to add tax preparation services to my business	_____
Practice Management		
○1　○2　○3	My business is too reliant on me being the rainmaker (if I died, it would die with me)	_____
○1　○2　○3	I need a career path and compensation plan for advisors in my firm	_____
○1　○2　○3	I want to get better at managing my time effectively	_____
○1　○2　○3	I can't seem to keep good people (high turnover)	_____
○1　○2　○3	The technology to run my business needs to be improved	_____
○1　○2　○3	My team has a clear structure of their roles and responsibilites	_____
○1　○2　○3	I need to hire an advisor	_____
○1　○2　○3	I need to hire an ops/support person	_____
○1　○2　○3	I need training for my staff	_____
○1　○2　○3	My gross revenue is good, but net profit is not where I want it to be	_____
○1　○2　○3	Other	_____

Image III.1: Challenges and Priorities Ranking Worksheet

ADDITIONAL RMM BUILDING BLOCKS

Now that you've identified your challenges and priorities, it's time to explore all the resources we've created to help you and your team fill in all the gaps in your practice to achieve ultimate operating capacity in the following areas: **holistic planning**, **marketing**, **profitable business lines**, and **practice management**.

HOLISTIC PLANNING

We've been running and fine-tuning the holistic planning process for many years and have worked really hard to turn it into a true plug-and-play system. By taking advantage of our programs, advisors all over the country have successfully taken their practices to new levels, offering a higher caliber of holistic planning and increasing the number of assets gathered, all while doing what's in the best interests of their clients. We've got scores of processes and models in three different areas of holistic planning: The Bucket Plan, the Tax Management Journey, and High Net Worth/Advanced Planning Strategies, as follows:

The Bucket Plan

By this point in your career, you've probably been successfully doing some form of bucket planning in your practice for quite a while. To help advisors like you be even more effective, we've developed proven processes, techniques, props, and tools that you can begin using today to not only increase profitability but also add value for your clients. Achieving greater buy-in and forming lasting connections with prospects and clients, running seamless bucket planning meetings in person and virtually, educating your clients about money and risk so that you can capture more opportunities than ever before, creating family succession plans that help you retain assets across generations, and providing an extra layer of protection and proof of documentation that you followed a best interest fiduciary process to create your holistic plans—we cover it all.

The Tax Management Journey®

These modules give you the competency and the confidence to implement critical tax management strategies with your clients to deliver superior planning. By mastering this track you will differentiate yourself from other advisors in your community, giving you a big advantage over the competition and helping you win more business as a result. Our training, tools, and resources on the following important topics will get you there. You'll learn simple ways to educate your clients about using tax-efficient funnels to fill their buckets, and the importance of diversification and tax-sensitive distribution strategies. You'll learn how to measure and understand tax brackets, avoid marginal tax traps, minimize required minimum distributions (RMDs), understand and describe gifting strategies, and take the tax bite out of capital gains. And since the tax code is so dynamic, we have on-demand e-Learning that's updated as conditions change, as well as client-facing tools, point-of-sale resources, all the materials necessary to deliver successful consumer seminars on taxes, and access to an online training that will help you become a better public speaker.

High Net Worth (HNW)/Advanced Planning Strategies

Here you'll get a detailed overview of the Family Estate Organizer (including tips, tools, and best practices) and learn how to communicate the benefits to the clients and prospects to whom you offer this value-added service. Administrative support is critical to implementing the Family Estate Organizer, so we also offer step-by-step instruction for the people who assist you in creating them for your clients. And since taxes are of such concern to HNW clients, there's a module that teaches you how to read and understand a tax return, as well as a guide to reverse mortgages.

MARKETING PROGRAMS

Of all the types of support we offer to advisors through C2P, the most often requested is help with marketing. So many of us struggle with how best to spend our time and marketing resources, and choosing which marketing path(s) to follow seems like a total crap shoot. It doesn't have to be that way. Through our marketing programs and training—which were created by some of the brightest marketing minds in our industry—advisors are learning how to craft and implement plans and strategies that truly make the most of their limited time and budgets and get them in front of more ideal prospects than ever before. Take a look at this lineup of stellar opportunities on marketing planning and strategy, digital marketing, virtual and in-person seminars, and referral systems, all of which are designed to take your marketing efforts to the next level.

Marketing Planning and Strategy

These modules cover everything you need to effectively market to your existing clients, reach new prospects, strengthen relationships with your centers of influence, build your brand, and create recognition through the use of media including television, radio, and print. There's a turnkey program for an innovative, cost-effective golf marketing solution designed to filter and target ideal prospects and build your local brand *without any direct mail costs.* As described in Part II, we've created a process for forming alliances with attorneys to turbocharge your referrals, increase credibility, and bridge the critical gap between two essential planning areas while splitting the marketing costs between you and other like-minded professionals. And you can access a module that teaches you how to create your own strategic marketing plan, with a template and scorecard included!

Digital Marketing

Whether you're being forced to operate virtually because of a pandemic or you just want to develop a variety of ways to engage with prospects and clients, this training will provide you with tips and tricks for doing it effectively. You'll learn how to set up your computer, which software to use, camera placement (including how to use multiple cameras), and the most effective ways to communicate virtually. If you ever dreamed of being a radio star when you were a kid, there's even a turnkey podcast marketing system.

Virtual and In-Person Seminars

Seminars can be a highly successful form of marketing. Watch top advisors execute actual seminars on topics like The Bucket Plan, estate planning, Social Security benefit options, tax planning, and so on, and learn tips, tricks, and best practices for making presentations that really stick. You'll also gain access to our extensive seminar content resources, which include sample invitations and tickets, customizable presentation decks, props, workbooks, and scripts. You'll learn what makes people buy, how to gain trust and book more appointments, five steps to giving a great presentation, how to prescreen for affluent clients, how to book appointments and avoid cancellations, the emotional dynamic of communicating with groups, and how to mesmerize an audience through storytelling. And since people of retirement age are confused about Social Security and are actively seeking help in navigating this complicated system, we take you through all the steps to become a trusted Social Security consultant, giving you the educational materials and resources to gain the necessary knowledge and also market your services, host workshops, set appointments, and run the actual consultation process.

Referral Systems

If you're like many advisors, you are uncomfortable asking for referrals—but referrals are critical to your business's growth. These modules show you various ways to get referrals without having to grovel. You'll learn how to use a simple survey to get your clients to raise their hands and voluntarily offer to refer others to you, and a step-by-step process for how to turn those referrals into clients. There's even a training for your marketing coordinator to get returned calls and build confidence to overcome any objection to your calendar week after week.

PROFITABLE BUSINESS LINES

We speak to our clients every day about the need for diversification in their portfolios. Diversification is a necessity for mitigating risk and managing volatility . . . we all know that. Yet all too often we fail to apply the diversification principle to ourselves. Having a practice that's reliant solely on AUM is extremely risky because what if the market crashes? You don't want to be solely reliant on insurance either. Not only are you not doing holistic planning by not offering both, but you're also missing a big opportunity to diversify your revenue streams. This is why we created the following modules on Building or Buying a Tax Practice, Adding a Medicare Practice, and Insurance and AUM Building Strategies to help you grow by building additional profitable business lines into your practice. Having these tools in your toolbox rounds out your holistic planning and gives you the ability to add more revenue streams to your firm.

Building or Buying a Tax Practice

Create a new base of clients by integrating tax planning, management, and preparation services into your financial advisory firm using this proven eight-step client acquisition process. Learn how to add a tax professional to your office (everything from placing the right kind of ad to onboarding and training), and discover the art of transforming a tax client into a financial services client.

Adding a Medicare Practice

Insource expertise and capability with our powerful 10k Boomers a Day* Medicare supplement marketing program. With information from this module, you will learn how to hire and promote a skilled insurance agent onto your team and build a stream of leads for your financial advising practice quickly, easily, and cost effectively.

Insurance and AUM Building Strategies

In these powerful modules, you'll learn about our algorithmic annuity product screening process and product shelves, as well as receive a guide for how to use them. There's training that teaches you how to overcome the various objections to fixed index annuities by providing comparisons to variable annuities, case studies, and numerous articles, charts, and videos that you can share with your clients, and you'll learn how best to implement fixed indexed annuities (FIAs) in your clients' Soon and Later buckets. You'll find new ways to uncover financial planning opportunities while reviewing a client's or prospect's tax return. You'll discover how our turnkey asset management provider can help you deliver a superior investment experience through a single connected platform, and how our RIA, Prosperity Capital Advisors, can enhance your business.

PRACTICE MANAGEMENT

During our preparation to become financial services professionals, we rarely, if ever, are offered any meaningful training on how to manage a practice effectively. This is unfortunate because it negatively affects our ability to give great service to our clients and grow our businesses for the long haul. Practice management is something that many advisors struggle with constantly. It is undoubtedly the hardest thing to learn on your own. For that reason, we partnered with some of the brightest minds in our industry to develop a suite of trainings, resources, and tools on mergers and acquisitions, advisor career path and compensation, and business operation and efficiency to help rainmakers build and manage their holistic wealth management practices in a process-driven way that allows them to focus on what they do best—business development and creating great holistic plans for their clients. How to bring in new advisors and support staff . . . analyze cash flow . . . build a team culture . . . foster accountability . . . measure client profitability to enhance earnings, and so on—it's all right here.

Mergers and Acquisitions

If you're interested in growing your practice by acquisition, this module is for you. We have created step-by-step resources to guide you toward finding and acquiring businesses to help you achieve your ultimate growth goals.

Advisor Career Path and Compensation

Here you will learn how to leverage the talent on your team, develop financial advisors in the backstage, and define the mentorship approach that works best for your business. We cover everything from creating and posting job ads that attract your ideal candidates, identifying the right type of advisor for your firm, onboarding and training best practices, and we offer a wealth of supporting documentation to guide you through every step of the process.

Business Operation and Efficiency

Efficiency leads to profitability, and that's what these modules are all about. You'll learn how to gather and enter data into a template that will help you evaluate your current revenue, determine new lines of business that can boost your profitability, and analyze expenses to improve your bottom line. We've created a document that helps you easily track, capture, and create upsell opportunities as well as identify opportunities to cross-sell and gain more referrals. You'll learn how to run your practice like a well-oiled machine by improving communication, delegation, and time management. To help you determine your client profitability, there's an audit tool to discover what it's costing you to provide service levels and client touches in your practice. Since time is such a valuable and limited resource, we've created a system to help you and your team maximize your time within each day of the week. And you will learn how to mitigate your busy schedule while quickly and effectively qualifying prospects and properly identifying the appropriate advisor with whom the prospect should meet. We even provide the templates and scripts for making both warm and cold calls.

Find many of these RMM resources and additional information to grow your business at **RMMbook.com/toolkit**!

An Invitation

At this point you might be a little overwhelmed. Thinking about all the processes and systems you could add to your business is kind of like drinking out of a firehose. So, let's help you clarify your next steps. I want you to go back to the Challenges and Priorities Worksheet you completed and take another look at your rankings. On a sheet of paper, write down all the things you ranked as 1s and 2s. If you have more than five of them, you need to whittle that list down and make it more focused. Like I always say, if *everything* is important, then *nothing* is important. So study the list and figure out which are your top five challenges. *What are no more than five things that would make the biggest difference in multiplying your capacity as a rainmaker if you started working on them today?* Draw a star beside those and make the commitment that you and your team are going to embrace them as your "rock(s)"—your main initiatives going forward.

Now that you've got your rock(s), you have another decision to make: Are you going to embrace these initiatives by yourself, or are you going to get some help? You certainly can go it alone if you want to. I'm confident that you can do this!

Still, as I think about you navigating this path on your own, I can't help recalling my first trip to Prague with Pablo. With great excitement and anticipation, we set out walking the first day with the goal of catching all the must-see sights. We stumbled around that massive city for hours before realizing that we'd been going in circles the whole time. Exhausted, cranky, and overwhelmed, we realized that we'd seen only a fraction of what was there. We returned to the hotel in disappointment.

The next day we decided to try again, but this time, instead of going out by ourselves, we booked a professional tour guide to walk with us. What a difference! We got to see all the most important places with our guide explaining the significance of everything we saw, greatly enhancing our visit. Not only that . . . we saw three times the sites in half the time!

This brings me back to you. Like I said before, you *could* make this complex RMM journey on your own. But why would you go that route when you could call on a professional tour guide—the seasoned team at C2P—to walk you through it . . . to show you the way . . . to answer all your questions and prevent you from going in circles? You'll get so much more out of the trip (and in so much less time) if you let us help you. We have world-class support and learning systems in place to guide you including e-Learning, coaching, live and virtual training, model offices you can visit, industry-leading mentors you can access through our MentorCONNECT portal, and live Mastermind Collegiums where like-minded advisors share best practices and camaraderie and help each other grow. Whatever you need to start moving toward your goal, we'll be with you every step of the way until you achieve it.

Visit **www.RMMbook.com/toolkit** to schedule a free consultation to talk about how we can help you grow your business.

Thank you so much for reading this book and being part of my RMM journey. I can't wait to meet you on the road to building your self-sustaining holistic business and reaching new levels of success!

Acknowledgments

I have so many people to thank for their help—not just with this book but also with my business and my life.

I want to start with my wife, Holly, and the kids. Thank you for literally *everything*. I don't care if it sounds cliché, I am going to say it anyway: I could lose every material thing I have, and as long as I still had you, I'd be the richest man on earth. You are my anchor and my sails.

I want to acknowledge my parents for laying the foundation that made me the fiduciary financial advisor I am today. My mom taught me to always tell the truth, do the right thing, and live by the Golden Rule. My father—may he rest in peace—taught me so many things, not only about the insurance industry but also about entrepreneurism, perseverance, and hard work. He always said that if you're going to do something, do it right the first time—great advice that has served me well. Thank you, Mom and Dad.

My oldest brother Jerry's influence played a big role in the development of the Family Estate Organizer. Jerry, I learned so much from you, especially early in my career when I really needed your guidance.

Jennifer Mackert was the firm's first nonfamily employee. She was overqualified but made a big leap of faith in joining Holly and me when we were just getting started. She ultimately built and delivered the first financial plan for which we were paid a planning fee at JL Smith. Thanks for getting the ball rolling, Jennifer!

Pablo Terra, the best man in my wedding, took a similar leap of faith. He stepped away from a successful corporate career to become an entrepreneur with me in the start-up of C2P. Pablo, you're the glue that holds it all together.

Founding partner Dave Alison gave up the sunny beaches of Florida to live in the basement of my house in Cleveland—in the winter—to help us start up C2P. As they say, the rest is history. We couldn't have done this without you, Dave.

Don Chamberlin bought into the holistic planning model, saw the future of it, and joined me as a founding partner of C2P. I've leaned on your wisdom more times than I can count, Don. Thank you for your generosity.

John Del Greco also joined C2P as a founding partner and has been a wonderful mentor through all these years. He's taught me so much about people and relationships. John, you know that my eyes are always hugging you!

Carl Smith brought a thriving tax practice to our business model, as well as his unique ability to develop and foster relationships. Carl, you were a major key to our success.

Gina Pellegrini, a coach at Strategic Coach, was someone I looked up to. I never thought in a million years that she would join me as a partner in C2P as we were getting started. But she did. Thank you, Gina, for believing in the vision and being instrumental in developing the practice management resources we offer to the advisors.

Jeff Warnkin played an instrumental role in building JL Smith into the self-sustaining company it is today. Meeting him was a turning point in my life. Jeff, you're the best gentleman farmer I've ever known!

And of course there's Bryan Bibbo, who not only followed our process but worked harder than anyone to achieve the monumental levels of success that he enjoys today as a partner at JL Smith. You are a rock star, Bryan; I have learned so much from you.

Without Dan Sullivan's Strategic Coach program and Ed Slott's lead IRA advisor group, I am confident that the RMM Proven Process and Platform wouldn't exist. Dan and Ed, my gratitude to you knows no bounds.

And finally, special thanks to the remaining partners and amazing team members at JL Smith and C2P. You truly are the best in the business. I can't wait to see what we will achieve together in the years to come! Yuly Arcila, Jeannette Bajalia, Amanda Bibbo, Linda Biscup, Alec Bredel, Evelyn Bruce, Caleb Burr, Michael Cooke, Nikki Glynn, Justin Grossman, Cliff Guthrie, Jasmine Hamilton, Christine Kellogg, Kelli Knudsen, Rob LaCivita, Kara McClean, Seth Meisler, Olga Meys, Gary Pelfrey, Steven Phillips, Wade Quintana, Lee Sasser, Suzanne Scheiman, Farrin Schetter, Shelly Spieth, Maria Sullivan, Cathy Vincent, Joseph Voellm, Sarah Warnkin, Chad Weigl, Matthew Yakimow, Walter Young; Linda Aguila, Matt Alison, Dustin Anaas, Ryan Asher, Wayne Barker, Melissa Barrett, Kevin Beard, Loren Beck, Melissa Bridgman, Allison Bruckner, Cary Chaitoff, Kerry Darrington, Elaine DeStephano, Anthony DiPiero, Karin DiSanto, Samantha Doerr, Josh Dunaway, Cindy Frederick, Rob Ghosh, Dina Giavroutas Kachevas, Alex Green, Maddy Grimm, Greg Hammer, Michelle Hayes, Andrei Henson, Jailyn Jackson, Madison Johnson, Jeannie Kidera, Doug King, Alana Kohl, Chelsea Konst, Dennis Kyle, Leslie LaCook, Eric Langenfeld,

Angela Lavinski, Brenda LeBlanc, Gwen Lindsey, Kalem Mackey, Brian Mann, Karen Manning, Mike Mazzolini, Maebh McGowan-Doyle, Morgan Metzger, Gina Moravec, Erin Moser, Alex Mott, Clint Pelfrey, Stoyan Petev, Kai Prior, Bryon Rice, Luke Ripienski, Natalie Ripienski, Ben Roy, Barb Sawyer, Kirsten Schlumbohm, Alexandra Schmitt, Matt Seitz, Desiree Sgro, Casey Shaw, Missy Shermer, Jordan Smith, Sarah-Day Snipas, Bill Starken, Mary Sterk, Cassandra Tolin, Ryan Warner, Dillon Wilde.

Resources and Recommended Reading

The following books, thought leaders, programs, and organizations have been highly influential in my career and in my life. I highly recommend checking them out. I've also included my own books as recommended reading as you strive to build your self-sustaining practice.

Books and Programs by Dan Sullivan

- Strategic Coach Business Coaching: www.StrategicCoach.com
- *Who Not How: The Formula to Achieve Bigger Goals Through Accelerating Teamwork* (with Ben Hardy)
- *The Dan Sullivan Question: Ask It and Transform Anyone's Future*

Books by Patrick Lencioni

- *The Advantage: Why Organizational Health Trumps Everything Else in Business*

- *Getting Naked: A Business Fable About Shedding the Three Fears That Sabotage Client Loyalty*

Books and Programs by Michael Gerber

- E-Myth Business Coaching: www.EMyth.com
- *The E-Myth*
- *The E-Myth Revisited: Why Most Small Businesses Don't Work and What to Do About It*

www.PremierNSSA.com

- Social Security consulting education

www.IRAHelp.com/advisor-training

- Ed Slott's tax planning training

www.MDRT.org

- Million Dollar Round Table Top of the Table offers great exposure to thought leadership and anything your business needs in the coming year.

www.FrontRowDads.com

- I highly recommend this organization for family men who are also high-performing entrepreneurs.

Books and Conferences by Verne Harnish

- *Scaling Up: How a Few Companies Make It and Why the Rest Don't (Mastering the Rockefeller Habits 2.0)*
- Attend Verne's summits and workshops for a high-energy injection of his outstanding principles: https://scalingup .com/summits/.

- www.EOSWorldwide.com
- Entrepreneurial Operating System (EOS) helps entrepreneurs like you and me "eliminate our business-related frustrations, get what we want from our business, and live our ideal lives." Highly recommended.

Books by Jason L Smith

- *The Hiring Advantage: Three Simple Steps to Streamline and Enhance the Hiring Process in Your Financial Services Practice* (with Gina Pellegrini)
- *The Bucket Plan: Protecting and Growing Your Assets for a Worry-Free Retirement*
- *Days Can Be Sunny for Bunnies and Money* (children's book with Tish Rabe)

About the Author

JASON L SMITH is a father, husband, nationally acclaimed speaker, financial planner, best-selling author, coach, and entrepreneur. Following in his father's footsteps as a second-generation advisor, he founded his holistic wealth management practice, JL Smith Holistic Wealth Management. His firm offers services that combine the five pillars of holistic wealth management—financial planning, asset management, tax management, protection planning, and legacy planning—into one comprehensive, coordinated plan.

At JL Smith, Jason built a self-sustaining model where his practice can run with or without him. His passion is sharing this business model with other advisors to help them grow by walking them through the Rainmaker Multiplier Proven Process and Platform.

With the overriding goal of simplifying financial planning for 1 billion people worldwide, Jason founded C2P—offering investment, insurance, and training solutions for holistic financial advisors—and Prosperity Capital Advisors, an award-winning SEC-registered investment advisory firm. Through these organizations, he utilizes his experiences as a highly accomplished advisor to train other advisors through live training events, educational content, and coaching calls.

The Bucket Plan: Protecting and Growing Your Assets for a Worry-Free Retirement was Jason's first book and a bestseller that has received top accolades from publications such as *U.S. News & World Report* and entrepreneur.com.

Jason is a regular speaker at industry events such as SHIFT and Million Dollar Round Table (MDRT). Additionally, in 2015 Jason was recognized as one of *Investment News*'s 40 Under 40 and named to Crain's Notable Wealth Managers list. He is often cited in industry and national media discussing the importance of providing holistic financial services.

About Clarity 2 Prosperity

Clarity 2 Prosperity is a financial training, coaching, and IP development organization that offers financial advisors turnkey financial planning, practice management, and marketing processes. Our mission is to help advisors shift from a transactional mindset to being a holistic planner who offers best interest advice by coordinating all areas of their clients' financial lives including investments, insurance, tax, estate, Social Security, retirement income, and health-care planning.

To achieve this mission, we provide live, on-demand, group, and one-on-one training along with tools, resources, mentoring, and support to ensure successful implementation of our packaged proven processes, including The Bucket Plan® Best Interest Process and the Rainmaker Multiplier.

For more information, visit us at www.Clarity2Prosperity.com or call (888) 240-1923.